The Great Brexit Exit

The Great Brexit Exit

Upping roots, leaving the country……
two novice caravanners and a dog
eloping to the Canaries
(in a pandemic/amidst Brexit)

by
Lisa Holmes

Copyright © 2021 Lisa Holmes

All rights reserved. No part of this book may be reproduced or used without written permission of the copyright owner except for the use of brief quotations.

FIRST EDITION 2021

Paperback ISBN: 978-1-80227-288-8
eBook ISBN: 978-1-80227-289-5

Table of Contents

Tenerife—here's the why! 1

Friday 23rd October: Packed up by container company— 8 a.m. to 4 p.m. 18

He broke it before we got started……… 20

Saturday 24th October 2020: Harwich 22

Hoek van Holland—Docked at 4.45 p.m. 24

Sunday 25th October: Nazareth, France 29

Monday 26th October: Roye, France 33

Paris next—domination! 36

Paris 37

Tuesday 27th October: Niort/Doeuil-sur-le-Mignon, France 38

Wednesday 28th October: Saint-Jean-d'Angely, France 39

Thursday 29th October: Saint-Jean-de-Luz, France 43

Oiartzun, Basque Country, Spain 44

Zaldibar/Berriz/Abadino/Lurreta/Amorebieta-Etxano/Muskiz/Castro-Urdiales/Cabuerniga, Spain 45

Friday 30th October: Cabuerniga, Spain 48

Saturday 31st October 49

Sunday 1st November: Left Cabuerniga, travelled through Cieza/Reinosa, Spain 50

Monday 2nd November 54

Tuesday 3rd November: Leaving Reinosa, Spain. Travelled through Coria del Rio	60
Wednesday 4th November	63
Thursday 5th November: Conil de la Frontera, Spain	64
Friday 6th November	66
Saturday 7th November	68
Sunday 8th November	69
Monday 9th November	70
Tuesday 10th November: Leaving day… We travelled to Cadiz port through Andalusia and Seville	70
Wednesday 11th November	73
Thursday 12th November	74
Friday 13th November	76
Saturday 14th November	78
Sunday 15th November	78
Monday 16th November	79
Tuesday 17th November	81
Wednesday 18th November	82
Thursday 19th November	84
Friday 20th November	87
Saturday 21st November	90
Sunday 22nd November	91
Monday 23rd November	92
Tuesday 24th November	94
Wednesday 25th November	95

Thursday 26th November	95
Friday 27th November	96
Monday 7th December	99
Thursday 10th December	100
Friday 11th December	100
Wednesday 16th December	103
Friday 18th December	103
Monday 21st December	104
Tuesday 22nd December	104
Friday 25th December 2020	104
8th January 2021	105
5th January 2021	107
11th February 2021	109
5th March 2021	110
14th April 2021	110
26th April	111
30th April—1st May	112
20th May 2021	112
27th May	113
Tuesday 1st June 2021	117
4th June 2021	118
13th June 2021	118
Wednesday 23rd June	119
20th July 2021	122
16th/17th/18th August	122

Tenerife—here's the why!

Clive and I met in early 2015. He moved from Guiseley, West Yorkshire, and me, from East Tilbury, Essex to live together. We found affordable accommodation at St. Osyth, just outside Clacton-on-Sea, Essex. We rented a small chalet-type building which had just been renovated so it was clean, tidy and furnished. It had two very small bedrooms, a living room and kitchen combined, a spacious bathroom with bath, toilet and sink and a cupboard which housed the fixings to plumb in a washing machine, which we later secured second-hand. The furniture, a two-seater sofa, one armchair, a double bed, fridge and cooker were brand new. It was ideal as all we had when we got together were the clothes on our backs and Clive's work van containing all his carpentry tools. The chalet was at Bel Air Estate which was somewhat unsavoury. There was a large element of grinding poverty within the area. The majority of people had nothing; no hope, no money, no real future. They lived week to week, giro to giro. This poverty caused a lot of stress and aggression amongst the dwellings within which we found ourselves. I was not comfortable in this setting at all.

    Clive found work reasonably quickly at Clacton Pier. He really enjoyed it there but the pay was far from what he had experienced previously. He brought home £280 a week which kept us ticking over. I struggled to find work, and, with no car and as there was no train station, getting out of St. Osyth by bus limited my job prospects enormously. Most people had motorbikes or bicycles if they were not flush enough to own a car.

As summer became autumn and the weather really started to plummet into the depths of freezing, bitter cold, we decided we had no choice but to leave and find something with central heating and insulated walls. The only heating we had then was a Calor gas fire which we purchased and this was far from suitable. It needed to be on all the time we were at home and it was very smelly in our small confines which caused serious condensation, something we were already experiencing beyond our control. Mould was evident on all the walls, growing like sponges in some areas and black inky grime in others. Mould sprays were no more than a short-term treatment, banishing it for a day or two. I even tried neat bleach; that too was disappointing but smelt better than the alternative. It was time to make a hasty departure.

We found a bungalow in Jaywick, newly renovated since its previous tenants, being involved in drug dealing, had been directly responsible for the property almost being burnt to the ground. The owner had just finished having the place rebuilt and totally redecorated inside. There was gas central heating and all mod cons including a huge bathroom which the previous chalet could almost have fitted into. However, it was empty, devoid of any furniture, bed, cooker, fridge, anything. We sourced most things second-hand. We managed to get a brand-new bed from an opportunist who happened to be driving round the estate with an excess of stock! It was that familiar idiom… 'it fell off the back of a truck', but it was offloaded much more elegantly. Anyway, it was a bargain. Neither of us welcomed sleeping on a second-hand mattress. One of the charity-run second-hand shops in Clacton had some new white goods and we managed to get a brand-new fridge/freezer (although it was for a built-in kitchen cupboard which was of little consequence to me—new and clean won the day). The cooker came from our second most popular supplier, Argos. It was a bog-standard electric cooker with a ceramic hob, a steal at just over £250. We moved within a couple of days, relieved to be warm, comfortable, detached from neighbours and away from that depressing environment. This felt like bliss after spending 9 months at St. Osyth, being isolated with little to do.

Within a couple of weeks of moving, I secured a job at Home Bargains which was new to The Clacton Factory Outlet and Clive upgraded his income by getting work with Bellways. Things were looking up. I got my own little purple Nissan Micra, compliments of Clive, for ease of travelling to and from work which meant I was finally free. It was a steal at just under £2,000 and had low mileage thanks to the one previous lady owner. I loved it. Clive upgraded his old banger which was a Toyota HiAce as it was on its last legs and would spew a cloud of black smoke behind us whenever Clive deliberately put the pedal to the metal to deter annoying followers who were driving too close and trying to get into his back doors! Plus, you had to wipe your feet as you left his van, such was the residue build up. The roof was green with moss, the rest of the van being a dirty, off-white colour due to the lack of washing. It was in need of a fireman's hose being let loose inside to clean away the layers of dirt and grime.

Clive really couldn't see any problem with his beloved old, scratched, banged about companion. I, on the other hand, couldn't see much good. Specsavers really had a big job on their hands with us two. This time, he invested in a Nissan NV200 which was shiny bright white, clean inside and had that new car smell that only valeting can provide.

Our next adventure was a well-deserved holiday on the island of Tenerife to visit Clive's parents. We travelled together for our first holiday abroad in January 2017 and were welcomed by glorious weather, spectacular scenery and warm, inviting family. With each visit after that, it became harder to return home. Our chats about eloping became more frequent and more determined. It was something we both wanted and started working harder to achieve.

We were ready, mentally, to make the move in early 2020, after yet another wonderful holiday. Life in the UK seemed to drag, the daily routine was becoming lacklustre; the surrounding area where we lived in Jaywick, (known officially on finger posts as Jaywick Sands), just outside Clacton-on-Sea, was becoming more bleak and less appealing. The police appeared to have no control and the criminal element was more evident daily. Drugs and alcohol were prolific in the area and they seemed to be increasing rapidly. There was violence on the street right outside our bungalow on more than one occasion, and basic laws were being ignored. There was no pretence trying to hide it. You could smell weed everywhere you went. Drinking was observed whenever we walked the dogs in the early morning and late at night. The decision to move was becoming very easy. My car passenger window had been smashed twice. The first time, my dash camera was stolen, the second time, nothing was missing; it seemed to be wanton vandalism. Clive's wing mirror had been smashed twice. The first time, the whole mirror was smashed off and it was hanging on by the electric cables. The second time, his mirror glass was in pieces. I feared every day that someone was going to break into his Nissan van to steal his tools. Friends of ours who live a couple of roads down had their van broken into and rampaged. He too was a carpenter and all his tools were stolen leaving him unable to work. Also, two doors down from us, a neighbour's vehicle was attacked with a crowbar in broad daylight. Thieves had tried to pry the door open on his transit van, not once, but twice. Having failed the first time, they returned later in the day. Luckily, they didn't succeed but these incidents unnerved me significantly. One Friday evening during 2020, Clive heard noises in the street so he ventured outside to check and saw an unruly gang of youths wandering around and loitering. Clive approached them and was threatened but he stood his ground so they fled. By this time of the evening, it was dark, the street lights were switched off so everything looked normal. It wasn't until the following morning that the realisation sank in when we saw numerous people out on the street in both Willow Way and Meadow Way, standing and examining their vehicles. When we went out to see what was wrong, we were informed that a total of 16 tyres had been slashed the night before. The scum had even entered people's gardens to stab tyres. You couldn't have anything of any value as it was either broken into, vandalised or destroyed. I was starting to loathe it there despite the pull of our friends, the lovely beach and the fact that we were both employed in good jobs. I didn't want to stay anymore; I just didn't feel safe.

At the beginning of the year, we had our dogs vaccinated against rabies and got their passports ready for the trip. We had started off with Bramble, who was a beautiful Jack Russell/Patterdale cross. Then we rescued a Pug named Bruno. Clive looked into flying the dogs over but Bruno could not. This breed is prone to breathing difficulties, especially when under duress. To be honest, I hadn't even contemplated the idea of putting them in an aircraft hold. I think it would be too stressful for me, let alone them. Anywho, we had June in our heads as the moving MONTH. Then, bang! COVID struck in March and everything came to a standstill. Clive was out of work as a self-employed carpenter and, my job at Home Bargains went bonkers. It was easy to pick up extra shifts. The shop was rampaged daily for toilet rolls as everybody knows. Madness ensued. The lockdown and its rules were ignored both in the shop and surrounding areas, as people from as far as London flocked to Clacton to party on the beach and shop. Caravan parks opened even though they weren't supposed to; the plan to leave became even more pressing.

Clive's bit:—(Just a heads up...... Clive has his own observations in parts which I encouraged as I did not want this to be solely from my own perspective, so his input is crucial to the facts, so you will see more of these throughout), as follows:—

The lockdown enabled me to spend more time with the dogs than I would normally do and to train Bruno, the Pug, as he had no recall, no lead work and no experience outside the home. In fact, he had no social skills with other dogs or people since his life had previously consisted of either being thrown out in the garden all day or locked in a small kitchen. By the time we were ready to leave the UK, I could walk Bruno off the lead and he would come when called. He became altogether a different dog. He even learned to play with toys, and eventually with Bramble, playing tug of war. It was wonderful to see his enjoyment and playfulness.

So, with the onset of lockdown, moving MONTH was postponed. We really didn't think it was going to happen in 2020 once COVID took hold. Then, in June, we lost our beloved Bramble at the age of 11. I could still blubber now. We thought they were both coming on the exciting adventure we had planned but, tragically, she could not.

After the three-month lockdown had passed, Clive returned to work and things gradually returned to semi-normal so we decided to set our plan into action and make our move before Brexit caused any more issues with the move to Tenerife.

As soon as the house was sold and finalised in September 2020, we started seriously organising as this provided us with the funds to start afresh. We bought a caravan (£1,650.00), to take with us which would be cheaper than staying at B&B's or hotels, not that we had much choice with a dog in tow and COVID causing its own set of problems. To be honest, finding somewhere to stay overnight en route was going to be tough. Neither of us had ever embarked on anything like this before.

We had no idea what we were looking for when it came to the caravan. Clive had spent hours on the internet looking at caravans in varying degrees of age and condition. Some were ridiculous prices in relation to their poor state but people were taking advantage of COVID so, in some cases, prices were pushed beyond what they should be.

We went on instinct and hoped for the best. Luckily, we fell upon some lovely, genuine people who had a wonderful caravan, well looked after, and with lots of extras. It had a motor mover, which enabled you to move the caravan by remote control and to manoeuvre it into the desired position once it was removed from the towing hitch.

There were some very interesting gadgets inside. When you lowered the feet on the caravan to stabilize it, there was a spirit level in the front window to level it along its length and width. There was a lock that fitted over the towing hitch to prevent anyone just driving up, connecting it onto their vehicle and towing it away. There was a locking mechanism to put on one of the feet to stop people winding the foot up and taking it. It had a tv, stereo, gas bottles, water tanks and a large awning. The gas cooker looked brand new. It had a separate bathroom with a toilet, sink and shower cubicle. The cubicle was very tight for Clive. It didn't allow him to move about very much, let alone move his arms around to wash from head to toe. Clive is rather broad in the shoulders having lifted weights for the best part of his life, so, this was going to be a tight exercise for him. There was also a double wardrobe in this room. In fact, it was a reasonable-sized bathroom with lots of cupboard space under the sink and above at eye level. The manufacturers had certainly made use of every inch of available space to ensure you were well catered for. The kitchen had plenty of cupboard space with base units in between the fridge and cooker and at eye level. The fridge could either be run on gas or electricity. There was a cupboard at the far end where the two long sofa seats were. The tv was housed in this locking cupboard and underneath was a pull-out section with slats joined together with webbing. This joined the two sofas together to make a large double bed. All you had to do once this section was clicked into place was rearrange the cushions from the back of the sofas to fill the gap. Everything was actually perfect. First to view, first to buy. Wow, we really were going for it. We put a deposit on the caravan immediately as the market for caravans during the lockdown period had been going mad. People were taking up caravanning and staying in England due to travel restrictions. Some friends agreed to allow us to store the caravan on their property until we were ready to leave. This would give us time to clean inside and get everything ship-shape.

Clive bought a tow bar online and found someone local to fit it to his van. As soon as this was done, (Saturday 19th September 2020), we returned to collect the caravan and pay the outstanding balance. We were both quite nervous as this was a first.

The seller helped us to hook it up. Unfortunately, the wrong electrical fitting had been connected on the tow bar. We found out there are two types of connectors and, as it seemed to be the way with us, we chose the wrong connector, so we had to drive home without any brake lights or indicators on the caravan. That was an experience neither of us wanted to repeat. We were on the edge of our seats all the way home. We took a wrong turn which led us

The Great Brexit Exit

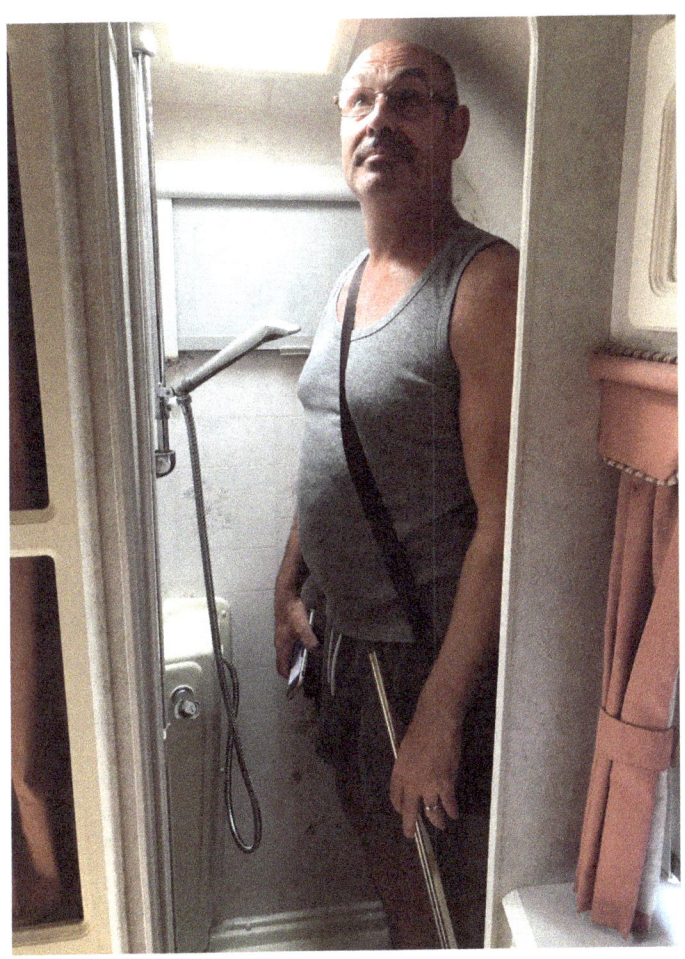

down a road with sleeping policemen—not good for towing a caravan. We were head-banging over every bump.

We decided to turn around. This ended up being a 50-point turn since we were both unfamiliar with reversing whilst towing something much bigger than the Nissan van Clive was driving. It was something of a beast, measuring 19 feet in length. It was a BIG caravan. It is much harder than you think reversing, requiring a fair amount of experience. By the time we got the caravan to our friends' property and packed away, we were both very uptight and needed a large glass of wine. The journey seemed to take forever. And this was just the start of the STRESSSSSS, I mean, adventure……

Clive's bit:—*Oh dear, never ever have I towed anything! I've driven small lorries and large vans, but this was completely out of my comfort zone. The van didn't respond like normal and the turning and rear view, or lack of it… oh no, I was totally unprepared, but Lisa told me to man up and get on with it. The hour's drive home left me shaking and in need of a stiff drink. It took my eyes and bladder about a week to return to normal.*

We sourced an adaptor for the electrical fitting from the van to the caravan so we had working lights. Thank heavens Homestead Caravans at Weeley was only a 10-minute drive away because it ended up being our second home during the next few weeks. Homestead had a service centre which we discovered far too late to take advantage of. We would have been quite happy to pay for a manual handling lesson. We certainly needed it. The caravan shop was well stocked with lots of goodies, both practical and essential. Every visit ended with us leaving, bags in hand, full with more purchases. I loved the place.

We cleaned the caravan throughout ready for our trip, filled the water containers and purchased full gas bottles which we hoped would fuel the whole journey.

Clive stopped me from going overboard and taking too much stuff because I would have packed everything. One item I had to leave was my collection of herbs and spices as he said I would not be allowed through Customs with such jewels—hmmm, I later regretted listening to him since some items cannot be sourced in Tenerife. As it happens, I would have been fine bringing all my herbs and spices but I didn't want to take a chance. The caravan was packed to the hilt. I wish we had been able to bring another trailer attached to the caravan but I fear Clive's Nissan van would have given up long before mainland Spain.

Clive's bit:—*Lisa needs things to be scrubbed within an inch of their life. We packed our bedding and our everyday stuff that we would need to survive our trip. Lisa also requires multiple foodstuffs—by that, I mean more than 3 of the same thing in the cupboards—and so these went in the caravan too.*

It is worth noting that you should check the electrical fitting on your caravan. I did not know there were two types of plugs connecting the electrics from the car to the caravan operating the brake lights and indicators. It is either 7 or 13 pins.

Over the next couple of weeks, we planned what needed to be in place. We paid up to the 23rd of October for all the utility bills, etc., at the bungalow we were renting. The Brexit Exit was underway.

We both handed in our notice. Clive didn't really have to as he was self-employed but was sub-contracting for a company so he let them know he was moving. Our last day at work was Friday 9th October 2020. We gave ourselves a week to get packed up and sort the caravan out. We planned to leave on 16th October. We booked a container as it was really the only option to bring all Clive's tools over. We tallied up their value to around £8,000.00 so they had to come with us. Various other 'can't live without' items got packed into the container. Well, we paid £3,500.00 for the container so we thought we might as well bring as much as we could to make it worthwhile.

The container company we started off with quickly turned sour. They kept adding to their original quote which was getting more and more ridiculous. Then, when we thought we had a final figure, they hit us with import tax; well, they were unsure of that value as we would not be residents at that point so this could be a big add-on.

We really didn't feel comfortable staying with them because of this and after reading pages of negative reviews, we decided to change companies at the last minute.

Global Moving Services were transparent from the off, quoting insurance and import fees so we knew exactly what the end cost would be. Because of the last-minute change, we had to adjust our leaving date as they didn't have a container available on the date we requested. We agreed collection from our property on Friday 24th October 2020, so, we had another week and a final date to work towards.

We organised the ferry journeys. Firstly, the short ferry with Stena from Harwich to the Hoek of Holland on Saturday 24th October, journey time 7 hours (£170.00), then the big one with Transmediterranea, Cadiz to Santa Cruz de Tenerife, which Clive booked online for two weeks after departure. However, as he confirmed this on-screen, the date changed to 1st November. (Journey time 41 hours—£997.00). This gave us a week to drive from the Hoek of Holland to Cadiz, some 1,441.8 miles. We quickly rearranged the second ferry after this unfortunate error. I thought it would have been a push to drive this distance in a week. I'm a born worrier so I had every synopsis of mishaps spinning around in my hectic brain.

I don't think either of us wanted the stress of travel, finding somewhere to stay overnight *and* taking into account any breakdown/problems which may be encountered squeezed into a very short period of time. After rescheduling, we had the new date of 10th November to work to. So, we would depart at Cadiz on the 10th, and arrive at Santa Cruz de Tenerife on 12th November. This now gave us almost three weeks to enjoy the journey rather than frantically race to Cadiz for our final ferry journey to Tenerife.

The 9th of October soon came around and we busied ourselves with sorting all of our belongings in the bungalow; stuff to take, possessions for the container and the reject pile consisting of charity shop and recycling.

We thought two weeks from finishing work to leaving the country would be ample time to sort through our things. Huh. What an underestimation. By the time the two guys turned up with the lorry to collect the container contents, we had almost given up the will to live. We ended up disposing of much more than we originally intended. It was far harder than I had anticipated to scale down and reorganise. It certainly isn't something we want to go through again.

We packed quite a lot into the caravan; plenty of clothes to keep us going, all the cookware we required plus food and various other essential items. In actual fact, considering it was our virgin voyage, we did exceptionally well. Being ever so slightly OCD, I did have very specific lists drawn up for everything we needed.

Friday 23rd October
Packed up by container company—
8 a.m. to 4 p.m.

It was hard work watching everything we had earmarked to be containerised, wrapped to within an inch of its life in layers of brown paper and packing tape, being carried out and skilfully packed into a truck. We couldn't help as this would have rendered the insurance invalid. What a long day the 23rd of October turned out to be. At one point, I was sent off by Clive to buy biscuits to go with the tea for the packers and, sadly, whilst I was away, most of Bruno's bedding and all of his toys were packed. One of the boots I was going to wear was missing. Arrrrghhhh. Another lesson learned. Don't leave three men in charge. Hide everything away that you want to take. Don't leave anything to chance!

> Clive's bit:—*I might say at this point that if Lisa had been allowed to put everything she wanted in the caravan, the van's wheels wouldn't be on the ground.*

All our world in a van and caravan ready to leave the country. Deep breath! And, if I'd had any, Valium would have been administered STAT!!

So, we waved goodbye to the two guys and the lorry around 4 p.m. We went and collected our caravan. We had to get it out of the barn with no more than a foot on either side of it for clearance. Clive let the trailer jack down too fast and the caravan hit the deck. The motor mover wasn't responding so he had to couple it onto the towbar of the van and carefully ease it out of the barn. For the second time since buying it, the caravan was being towed with Clive driving. I did not have the confidence to tow it. We got home, packed the last lot of stuff into the caravan then had a visit from some friends who came to say Bon Voyage. It was very emotional, a combination of sadness and happiness. When they left, I threw a pizza into the oven for our last supper and promptly burnt it. Clive had a slice or two. Mine went in the bin. I was at the end of my tether by now.

He broke it before we got started.........

To pack more stuff into the back of his Nissan van, Clive had to take the caravan off the towing hitch and drive it forward in order to access the double doors at the back. When he did this, he forgot to unhook the safety chain which engages the brakes on the caravan in the event of it coming loose from the vehicle towing it. The safety

chain snapped as he moved forward. I thought this was the beginning of the end. It was all over. I was far from impressed and, at this point, in tears. The day had been long, tiring, emotional, and now I felt our very sketchy plans were foiled. I assumed the brakes would be jammed on to stop the caravan from moving. Clive was, as usual, cool, calm and collected. "It'll be alreet" was his Yorkshire phrase. Lo and behold, it was. The caravan was put back on the tow bar and responded as we moved on with the first leg of our adventure. We drove the short journey from Jaywick Sands to Harwich. This took about 30/35 minutes and we travelled in a quiet, thoughtful hush. We parked in the Docks car park, put the legs down on the caravan, took Bruno for a walk, fed him and ourselves and then bedded down for the night in readiness for the ferry journey in the morning. I couldn't quite believe we had left and were here in one piece, caravan still attached. Unbelievable.

> Clive's bit:—T*his really was the maiden voyage for us as caravanners. Even though it was only half an hour up the road, we were off, trying to keep the speed down and no bouncing over bumps.*
>
> *When I was a younger man, I was in the Merchant Navy and customs officers were really strict so I said to Lisa that we had to be squeaky clean for any inspections which, to my surprise, never really happened.*

Saturday 24th October 2020
Harwich

We were up around 6 a.m. and I was feeling a combination of excitement and terror as butterflies danced around in my tummy. We walked Bruno around the car park in the dark with Big Larry lighting the way (Big Larry is one of our buys from Homestead, a compact LED torch with several settings, a must-have for any sort of camping journey as it turned night into day like lights around a football ground). We all had breakfast, cleaned away and got ready to leave. As soon as we saw movement in the docks, we made our way to the front of the queue ready to embark on the Stena Ferry. As we waited, we saw a steep bridge leading onto the ferry. I commented to Clive that it was far too steep to pull our large, heavy

The Great Brexit Exit

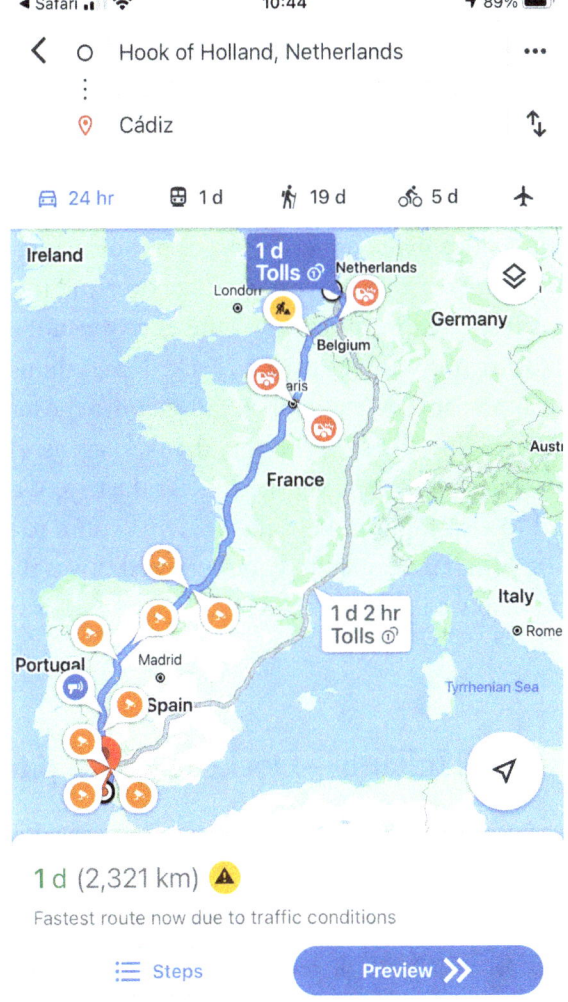

caravan up. He assured me that we wouldn't have to use that entrance. Hmmmmm. I was already worrying myself into a stupor. I'm my own worst enemy. As we waited, more caravans and cars started to appear. In fact, smaller caravans, which looked like proper two-berth caravans. The difference in size was so marked that we wondered whether we had chosen too big a caravan. Ours looked huge compared to all the others forming an orderly queue behind us. This made us very nervous but our choice was made, and pretty soon we were checked over and the caravan was inspected inside. Bruno's presence was not under any scrutiny nor were his papers checked even though we were well prepared. We were then moved onto the ferry by 9 a.m., avoiding the steep bridge, thank heavens. Bruno had to be put in a cage in the kennels for the trip. We were allowed to visit him but kept this to a minimum to avoid stressing him. He seemed to cope very well. I was the one crying when we left him there, but he just slept, it seems.

Hoek van Holland—Docked at 4.45 p.m.

The ferry journey was uneventful and boring. Basic foods and refreshments were available. We didn't book a cabin for either of the ferry journeys. This is something we regretted on this ferry. Seven hours didn't seem much on paper, but, in reality, it definitely was long and boring. Due to COVID restrictions, hardly anything was open which made the trip very tiresome. We came across a mobile phone charging unit whereby you inserted a Euro, plugged your mobile in and locked the cupboard to leave it charging. We thought a few hours would be sufficient to give us plenty of charge. We ended up leaving them there for over 4 hours to give them a good boost. When we returned to retrieve them just before the trip ended, our phones had charged a whole 2%. We were very disappointed; what was the point? This made our journey feel longer since we didn't have the luxury of playing games on our mobiles, watching TikTok or YouTube. This is something which became rather addictive to while away time. It would have been our only source of entertainment on a quiet, uneventful crossing if only they hadn't been in prison on a false charge.

We actually had to sit and converse with one another which seems to be a dying art. So, we decided to book a cabin as soon as we embarked on the journey from Cadiz. When Clive originally booked the ferry from Cadiz online, he thought the cabin price was rather expensive so we decided not to reserve one. Big, big mistake.

We arrived early in the evening in Holland and found a caravan park on Google where we could stay overnight, so we made our way there. After about two hours of driving on a wild goose chase, we were nowhere near a caravan site. The directions were very vague then the location would disappear. We pulled over in order to call some leads. We were advised that the sites were packing up for winter but were wished a sarcastic "Good luck", '(Taken-style)'. We looked at one another then at Bruno, the now salty sea dog, who grimaced knowingly. 'Ya should have planned it better. Even the idiot's sister asked if the route and stops had been planned.' Hmmmm. Our definition of "planning the trip" was to arrive in Holland and shove Cadiz into our iPhone's maps app and hey presto, the journey was planned. Easy. No maps, no engaging of brain cells, just listen and follow the instructions. Simple. To be fair, Clive had found an app map that had campsites all along the route but was unable to reactivate it when it was needed because it required roaming to be turned on, something we found out too late. Then COVID changed life, and, having the choke of Brexit around our necks, we knew this was going to be no simple task.

We ended up parking up for the night in a noisy lay-by on the motorway. There was nothing at all there in the way of toilets or showers, so we used our facilities. We were unsure of what to do with the water heater and shower procedure. This was more through ignorance than anything else and there was no manual to guide us through this.

Clive started the water heater which seemed to be responding nicely. We then got ready for the shower. Naked and cold, Clive embarked on showering first. He tried, in vain, to get water flowing from the showerhead. By the time he gave up trying, he was rather perturbed, cold and tired. I quickly boiled the kettle, filled up a bucket with warm water and gave him a plastic jug to get himself washed and rinsed. He did struggle in the small cubicle; I had to leave the bathroom to have a bit of a giggle at his squished antics, banging, crashing and grumbling. It sounded like a bull being manhandled into

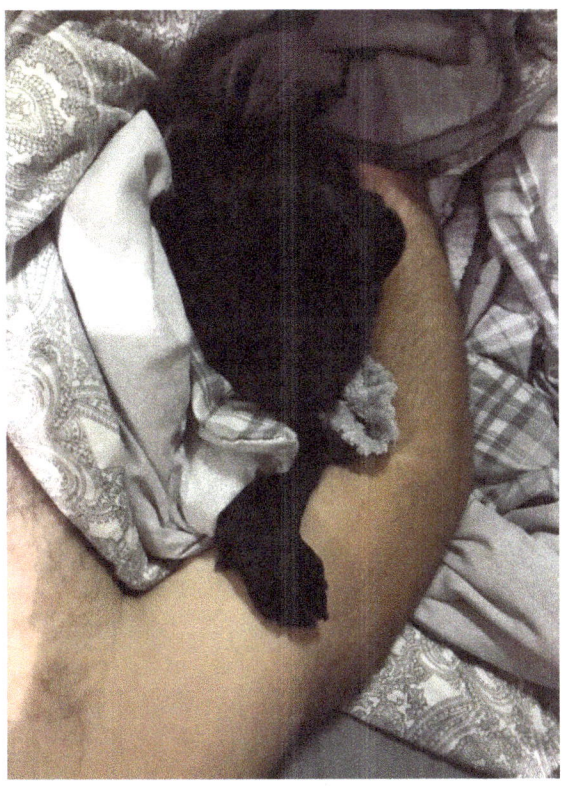

a crate. The air was blue. My turn next. I showered reasonably easy. The bucket and jug were not ideal but I felt clean and ready to climb into our freshly made-up bed after eating. Cheese and piccalilli sarnies with crinkle crisps for dinner. Very exotic but it filled a hole and enabled us to move onto sleepy time.

It was bloody freezing in the night. Bruno was on the bed with us, hidden under his fleecy blanket. It was so chilly we could see our breath. There was no messing on waking up and we dressed whilst the gas fire kept us warm. Between that and the cooker to boil our little bright blue whistling gas kettle—perfect. Those two being lit was sufficient to keep us comfortably warm until we moved on.

No caravan sites were open. We called quite a few but had no luck because I couldn't speak Hollandish or Frenchy. They were impatient and hung up. Then Clive tells me it's Dutch, not Hollandaise or Hollandish. Seriously, no one had any patience; as soon as we spoke English, bang, phone down. I was losing my patience very quickly too. Grrrrrrr!

Since travelling from the ferry at the Hoek of Holland, there had been nowhere to plug in our electrics. All of our technology was almost devoid of charge. The caravan battery was maintaining its charge as it received power from the van whilst driving. The only other thing being charged was Clive's mobile which we used as our satnav and this was plugged into the van's cigarette lighter. We were able to fill up with water at each stop but this was only for washing, not for our consumption. Luckily, Lidl and motorway services kept us going with bottled water. There were no shower blocks at the services so we had to use our own facilities.

On the positive 'YEE HAW' side, we were totally self-reliant. We had somewhat inflated egos at our resourcefulness. 'The Hunted' had nothing on us. Off-radar—oooooooooh, apart from the cameras at the services/Lidl/Peage tolls—OK, we're doomed, BUT… yes, a big butt, mainly from all the sitting—I had a good reason.

We had:—

- Used all the caravan facilities for cooking and heating, (needed—France in October—freezing cold, wet, windy—we had seen our breaths in the night and his crown jewels had shrivelled).
- Showered—although it was so small, Clive looked like Tom Hanks stuck in the floor in that scene out of 'The Money Pit'. Hilarious. And though we had a television and aerial, we were unsuccessful at tuning it in. Luckily, Clive had downloaded various films on his iPad before we left so we were able to occupy ourselves by watching a film late into the evening before bed. This was very handy.

All in all, a good experience in life. We laughed sooo much. Just as well because otherwise, I think one of us would be sporting a bump on the head or a very bruised ego.

Laughter is the best medicine and quickly diffuses stressful situations. So far................

Sunday 25th October
Nazareth, France

Day 1 on the road. We woke early at 6 a.m. and walked Bruno first before our morning brew. On our return, the whistling kettle went straight on and breakfast was sorted all round before setting off at 7.30 a.m. through Belgium and into France in search of a decent stopover. We picked up supplies and had cheese on toast for brunch in the caravan, which was most welcome and more enjoyable on the road than at home.

I'm not sure why that is but I used to find the same experiences were intensified on a sailing trip with my father. We would anchor offshore at the Black Water, Essex, where he had a caravan, spark up the Calor gas hob, throw eggs and bacon in a small pan, sit and inhale the mouth-watering smell, enhanced more by the sea air and the gentle rock of the waves, then sit in the cockpit filling our faces and sipping hot, sugary tea. Experiences are altered by sounds, smells, touch, taste, people and things and wonderful memories are forever etched in our minds. These memories, combined with other senses, are

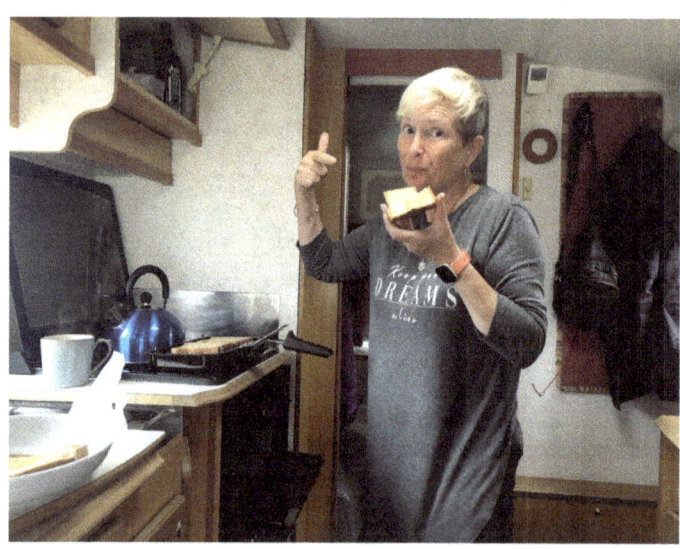

so much easier to pull on. They form a 3D memory for me that can carry me straight back to those joyful days.

We were cherishing the journey and slowly becoming caravan nerds. We travelled on and clocked up 240 miles that day. We were nearly in Paris. Bruno had been exceptionally well-behaved considering he had been imprisoned in the van and caravan since we left. His toilet breaks were regular but short-lived due to wet weather. It was a case of quick out, then back in the van, either in the footwell on a memory foam dog bed or on a blanky on my lap. He adapted well to travelling. It would have been a nightmare if he had been travel sick.

We stopped at another lorry park, one with toilets this time. The parking area was large with ample space to park our van and caravan as the spaces were specifically made for lorries. We had a shower but not in the conventional sense. The water heater worked fine supplying hot water at the kitchen sink but not continuing through to the shower. We discovered the heater was leaking so we had to boil water again. We decided to try an overhead camping shower bag which proved to be very awkward. I had bought it in case we had any difficulties with the shower. You had to fill it up with warm water then hang it over your head and turn a lever to allow the water to run out of a small shower head. The only place we could hang it in the shower cubicle was on a clothes rail which hung quite low and since Clive is a big fella and tall, it turned what should have been a pleasant experience into an unpleasant chore, one that he rushed through as quickly as possible. It sounded like he was having a fight in the shower. The language was terrible. Even Bruno learnt some new disturbing words.

> Clive's bit:—*I found I couldn't put two hands above my head at the same time because I would get wedged in. And so, washing my hair was a one-handed job and then I would have to crouch below where my chest level would be to rinse the soap out and I would get wedged again.*

We had a new pressure relief valve but the weather had been awful so we were waiting for it to improve before the repair could be addressed. It was still very cold so the fire was on at night and in the morning. Bruno stayed snuggled on the bed covered up and snoring his head off. We retired to bed at 9 p.m. The travelling was taking its toll. We had both been very tired and slept well in the caravan. It was cosy with the addition of the memory foam topper we added. You felt safe in there especially with the police doing their rounds every night. It seemed to be a regular thing there with the police driving through the lorry parks at night. That, too, was reassuring.

Our showering regime was now limited to the washing up bowl full of water and a jug. The overhead shower bag was too much like hard work. You had to partially squat to get under it which wasn't ideal if you needed to walk afterwards; not at all conducive to a semi-comfortable existence. Being sat in the van for the best part of the day travelling then squatting to shower……… Self-inflicted torture.

Monday 26th October
Roye, France

We were up early again before 6 a.m. We had made a bad choice of stopover. We were parked on the edge of the motorway in a long lay-by, Chunnel train on one side, the main Paris drag on the other. It was very noisy due to the constant trains and traffic rushing by quite close to us. Bruno slept better than us. I think he was running through fields excitedly. I know because he was using my legs to get purchase. Bless!

After our obligatory walk around the one tree and electrical pylon, all three of us had brekkie. The weather was still pants, preventing us from our usual 45-minute or so outing. At this point in the journey, the weather was twinned with England, namely, wintry, bleak, wet and grey. It was brass monkeys out there!

We located a Lidl which was a 9-minute journey away. We arrived promptly and ONLY had to wait an hour and 10 minutes until the 8.30 a.m. opening. Oh, the trepidation of a bargain shop! On the motorway/dual carriageway, it was extortionate—€2.60 per litre of milk, €5.00 for a sausage roll. The only big thing you don't take into account being novice caravanners is the amount of space you require to park a van towing a caravan. It's extensive. We needed at least two and a half LONG spaces to get comfortably parked. This wasn't always available, especially if you hit the supermarket at busy times. Luckily, we managed, not through precise planning mind, to get parked without too many difficulties. You just can't prepare yourself for the delights and horrors of towing a beast of a caravan.

It was quite busy in Lidl as soon as the doors opened. In fact, there was a queue of locals waiting with their trolleys before opening, ready for the off at their starting blocks. Most attacked the fresh baguette trays as they were being pushed out. As we meandered around the store, I found a small plush Disney toy that looked perfect for Bruno. When we tried to pay for it at the checkout, the till operator said something to us in French at such a fast pace, I think we would have had difficulty understanding him if we were fluent. He then discarded the Disney toy by tossing it, slightly aggressively, to one side, then gave us a stern look. I guess that was a 'no' for that purchase.

In hindsight, I think the toy had to be sold in conjunction with a DVD or something similar and therefore could not be purchased at the advertised price on its own. I certainly would not have been so miserable about the attempted transaction having worked at the till in Home Bargains. A simple explanation and smile would have sufficed, even though we would still be none the wiser, but a smile always helps.

That was our first experience of the short-tempered French, but sadly, it was not to be our last. They seem to have little time for foreigners, I felt. I guess the onus fell on us to learn at least the basics; note to self… check up on Google, common phrases before entering the unknown…

We stopped at Esso 'Ass', put our debit card in to extract fuel, chose the one needed but were slow to pick the correct nozzle so got timed out. The procedure had to be restarted. We spent €30.98, the receipt concurred, one transaction, the previous one was zero. I then checked my mobile banking app. Two transactions were debited from my account to the sum of €116.98 each. What? I rang my bank and they stopped both transactions. I only asked for the one to be stopped. I spent the next 48 hours thinking we would be captured by the police for not paying for the fuel. Eventually, after a couple of days and constantly checking my app, I saw the correct amount was withdrawn to the sum of €30.98. Phew, no prison sentence.

Clive's bit:—*This was my fault as I dithered about the fuel choice. It was the same case in most 'motorway' petrol stations; card payment was requested rather than cash because of the pandemic. Figuring out what was diesel when you had several to choose from took a moment, which the card machine didn't like.*

Paris next—domination!

Well, it certainly felt that way by the time we reached here. We felt we were dominating the journey at least!

> Tolls so far: Monday €11.00, €11.30
> Most of the tolls we paid in cash but when we ran low, we paid by card. I was a bit reluctant to use my card now, so, once we paid, I got into the habit of going straight onto my banking app to check it was right.
> My habits are rather consuming at times…
> We estimated approximately
> £500/600 in fuel. We will tally up at the end. On the up side, we were not paying any stopover costs so reckoned it should be relatively inexpensive.

Poor Bruno had been very bored. He was stuck in the footwell of the van or on my lap. No toys to play with when we're in the caravan as they were ALL packed away by mistake. We had to ad-lib. We found a small plastic funnel. He thought this was great fun as it kept pinging out of his extraordinarily small mouth all around the caravan. He seemed so chuffed that he had something to chase and try to chew. Ten minutes of play and he was snoring like a pig.

Paris

We hit the outer ring road. This was one of our biggest headaches ever. There were roadworks everywhere so we tootled along in first gear for an hour and a half with motorcycles weaving everywhere. Police cars and unmarked vans passed us regularly with their sirens whirring. There seemed to be an unusual amount of traffic around. I wasn't driving yet I was very stressed. It was my job to locate the next junction change. It felt like we had been on this road for 4 or more hours. It was a hard drive. Since arriving in Holland, we had travelled over 400 miles; the maximum speed was between 55-60 mph in the van towing a 19-foot caravan loaded to the hilt. High winds and rain hadn't helped. We later found out that Paris was being shut down, and people were struggling to escape.

Tolls—€35.00 and €40.00. Diesel today—€51.00 and €15.00. Hours driven—roughly 10. We had covered 580 miles. Hours remaining on the road—12.50.

Clive's bit:—*The outer ring road was absolute bumper to bumper. The motorway driving, to be fair, was relatively easy. France is flat. I had to keep a close eye on my speed as it was quite easy to climb past the speed allowed towing a caravan. The hardest parts to negotiate were the petrol stations and tolls as the space was limited. With the stations, it was rejoining traffic, getting up to speed. Tolls were a squeeze through the booths.*

After gathering supplies from a French Lidl, dinner was a very enjoyable mix of sausages, bacon, eggs, beans and French stick. We retired to bed early at 6.30 p.m. so we ended up waking early at 3 a.m., cold and in need of warmth. Clive walked Bruno quickly and hopped back into bed for a cuddle after a cuppa and a warm-up with the fire on. It really was bloody freezing at night. We naively thought it would have started to improve in temperature by then, but NO!

Tuesday 27th October
Niort/Doeuil-sur-le-Mignon, France

Another 6.30 a.m. rise. We had the loudest lorry next to us in the night. Probably cold storage as the engine was going all night. The parking area was extensive and provided extra-long bays for caravans right around the edge of the parking facility. The toilets and the whole area were clean and tidy. We were able to replenish our water supply for washing but not drinking water.

Having all had our early walk, then being fed and watered, we were off on our journey by 7.50 a.m.

We were on a straight 329-mile stretch of toll road. No seeing glasses to check for signs for a looooooong time. Yayyyy!

We made a detour to Lidl again as we needed more drinking water and food supplies. The fridge was great but the freezer compartment was not huge so we needed to buy meat products every couple of days. There was a hairy hairpin road to manoeuvre both vans through. That certainly makes you hold your breath and clench your sphincter. I didn't realise caravanning could be on the edge of your seat, verging on sh……g (pooping) yourself; anxiety overload. I would not be able to drive towing the caravan as it was far too scary and stressful for me and I was just a passenger experiencing this. Clive drove superbly, though, and took all these issues in his stride. He didn't seem to be at all stressed, I thought.

Wednesday 28th October
Saint-Jean-d'Angely, France

It was strange with someone else in the bed, snorting, snoring, snuffling, dribbling… then Bruno started!

Tolls—€5.00 and €20.00

More rain today. 40% chance… Yeah.

We awoke before 6 a.m. Got through our usual routine of walkies, breakfast and winding up the caravan feet to get moving on the road. We headed to a Laverie (launderette), as we were down to our last few pairs of knickers. 18 km (19-minute drive). We had a quick trip straight there, no tiny, awkward to manoeuvre roads, which was a godsend. The satnav seemed to be getting the hang of this navigation objective.

We arrived at an industrial-style shopping area. The small but well-equipped laundromat was surrounded by a huge hypermarket, brasserie, Mackey D's and Brico (hardware store)! The launderette was immaculate, very well equipped with the latest Electrolux industrial washers and dryers. We were very impressed with the cleanliness and service. Overall, France had provided excellent overnight parking facilities which were regularly spaced along the motorway, enjoyable travelling on the well-maintained roads, and impeccable services, whether they be shops or anything else. We concurred that the tolls were well worth paying if they provided all the amenities needed for a comfortable journey.

So, washing on, walk Bruno, next stop, shop. We had a good walk around as this shop provided a huge array of groceries. We picked up a nice assortment, got to the till and I noticed the person in front had bagged their loose items and priced them already. All our fresh items, i.e., potatoes and tomatoes, were loose. Blast! We had missed the scales and pricing bit. Back to the fresh produce. This was our second experience of feeling dumb and useless in a foreign country. Trying to figure out what was what. You would think it would be pretty basic. Pictures of items to choose from. Huh… 30 different options for tomatoes at least. I chose what I thought was right. Back to the till to be told in a stern French accent, 'N0N'. Clive went back while I waited with our shopping as most of it had already been scanned. The waiting French customers were frowning at me, impatiently tapping their trolley handles; I felt very embarrassed. Finally, Clive returned with a handful of stickers for the cashier to choose the right price. Four tomatoes for €2.67. What?

Next, we went on to the brasserie for freshly made baguettes, cappuccinos at Mackey D's and finally, we were all charged up and ready to go. We sat in the caravan, consumed our lovely baguettes, sipped the glorious coffee and relaxed for 10 minutes. We hadn't had a Mackey D's coffee for ages; it felt like years. It used to be a treat in the UK at the weekends on our way out for shopping. Large Cappuccino and the odd free one with all our saved stickers. This is something we had yet to encounter on our journey so far. Where were the stickers?!! Where were the large cups?!! One size fits all……… small, egg cup size. ☹

The sun was now shining and the temperature improving. No freezing in the night. We had clocked up over 700 miles and would shortly be travelling into Spain. 703 miles left. We were getting there.

Clive's bit:—*Lisa's face was a picture when she saw the laundromat. She does enjoy washing stuff.*

We settled down for the night at a large parking area with toilet blocks and outside taps for filling up our water supplies for washing. It was a beautiful wooded area and as soon as was possible after securing the legs in place and making sure the caravan was level, we took Bruno out for a long walk around the extensive green forest. It was beautiful there, quiet, clean and tidy, perfect for an overnight stay. Not far from where we parked, there were some wooden buildings with a lot of activities going on. It looked like a training area for something; we weren't quite sure what but they were quiet in their activities.

Thursday 29th October
Saint-Jean-de-Luz, France

Up at 6.30 a.m. According to the satnav, we had 10.11 hours left on our journey, equating to 703 miles.

Tolls paid today—€3.60, €2.65, €11.55.

We decided to try and find somewhere to stop over in order to have a proper shower but more importantly, to recharge all of our technology, mobiles, iPad, the main battery on the caravan which supplies lighting, the water pump, radio, tv (not that we were able to use this as we didn't successfully manage to tune it into any channels during the entire trip).

We stopped off to pick up a few supplies, mainly drinking water and a few fridge essentials, i.e., milk, cheese, bacon, etc. We collected what we needed from the store, and, as we were on our way back to the motorway, I saw a huge store where I thought we would be able to pick up a toy for Bruno. He was getting rather bored with his plastic funnel so, as it was starting to warm up and we didn't want to leave Bruno shut in the van, Clive sent me into the unknown entity that is a French hypermarket, alone. All I came out with after traipsing around and searching the whole place was the one dog toy, €8.00 poorer. He absolutely loved it. Just as well. I could have bought five toys from Home Bargains for that.

Oiartzun, Basque Country, Spain

We travelled roughly 100 miles through the Pyrenees mountain range into mainland Spain crossing the French/Spanish border. The Police were there in their numbers stopping various vehicles. We made it through unscathed. Phew, just as France went into lockdown, we seemed to be riding the wave of freedom.

France was basically as flat as your hat. We hit the Pyrenees, not literally, thank heavens, but shock, horror, suddenly there were huge inclines and descents around every corner which became very stressful when towing the caravan. The poor van was struggling somewhat up the mountains and then on the descents, you had to go very gingerly to avoid being propelled faster with the momentum of the sheer weight we were in charge of. We had to keep moving over into the slow lane with the big lorries flashing their hazards to say they were slow-moving. After a short spell, we decided to have a well-deserved break from the journey since we had made good time. Clive located a site with an English-speaking owner, who was most helpful and which, most importantly, was still OPEN!

Zaldibar/Berriz/Abadino/Lurreta/ Amorebieta-Etxano/Muskiz/Castro-Urdiales/Cabuerniga, Spain

It had to be the day the satnav insisted on the input of our location via postcode in order to navigate—the one minor detail we could not provide. After two failed attempts to follow the directions it gave us, which, incidentally, took us along the smallest roads and over the biggest speed bumps, I was losing the will to live. We passed a busy slip road on a bend and before we could move lanes, an imbecile driver was half on our lane, obviously a last-minute manoeuvre to take the exit on his part, putting us in a dangerous squeeze between a huge lorry and him, just making the fit by a hair's breadth. I needed a poo!

We stopped for fuel and the clever girls in the shop, even though they spoke no English but clearly understanding the situation, put the much-needed postcode into Clive's mobile so the satnav could chart the way to the caravan site. After a total of nearly four hours of trundling around, we arrived at the destination only to find fields with cows, sheep and a cute donkey. Clive rang the site and the very kind Spanish guy drove out to fetch us. We followed him back through some one-way country lanes to the site. It was absolutely beautiful. Shower blocks, toilet blocks, laundry room. Everything we needed. Plus, we had the pick of the pitches.

Clive's bit:—*In the UK, the postcode is a combination of letters and numbers. In Spain, it is 5 numbers and not only did I not know this, I was clueless and with no speaky (Spanish), I didn't have a clue how the girls at the petrol station figured out what I wanted, but they did. Thankfully…*

Bruno ran around the caravan like a lunatic. He didn't want to get back inside. We couldn't blame him since it was the first time he had been in the warm, dry, sun since leaving Harwich. He looked so happy and pleased to be outside that you couldn't help but smile at his antics. He had gone from salty sea dog to mountain goat. He decided that the zoomies around the outside of the caravan and fields were much more fun than being inside. We were all ecstatic, Bruno with his freedom, Clive for the break from driving and me, why wouldn't I be? I had a laundry, washing machine and dryer (not that I needed it with the beautiful weather), a fully equipped bathroom with power shower and electrical points for my hairdryer! Blisssssss!

This was the local supermarket, quaint and picturesque.

Clive repaired the leaking water heater by replacing the pressure relief valve. He fixed the flue for the gas fire which had come loose and the door seal as it had partially come off. We walked to the local shops, bought supplies, had a lovely homemade paella, a glass or two of wine, a power shower, film and a well-deserved relax in the quiet, idyllic, beautiful countryside resort. Snooooore…

Friday 30th October
Cabuerniga, Spain

We seemed to still be in work mode and up at silly o'clock most mornings. It was 6.30 a.m. today. We had a long walk exploring the area. Bruno made friends with a donkey. It was so sweet how the donkey just wanted to be close to Bruno. He wouldn't come anywhere near Clive or me.

We had music, electric, everything fully charged and everything that wasn't bolted down got washed and dried on the line outside. Considering it was the end of Octo-

ber, and being British, we are used to pretty poor weather at this time of year so we were astonished at how warm and glorious it was. This was what was needed right now, a few days to recharge and get everything cleaned up, the few repairs being taken care of ready for the next leg of the journey.

Saturday 31st October

We remained on site, exploring and enjoying the area and its beauty. The sun was shining and it was really warm. We felt absolutely spoilt to have the steaming hot power showers and all the modern facilities. How quickly you forget and take for granted everyday luxuries. It was nice to be reminded how lucky we were.

We met another couple on-site who were heading back to Devon today. They told us that there was an 18-mile tailback of traffic trying desperately to get out of France before it locked down. Paris was closed and we had just got out by the skin of our teeth. Places seemed to be locking down as we passed through. We had been very lucky not to be caught up in the middle of this pandemic. Because we had stayed on the main roads and spent the nights in lorry parks, we managed to steer clear of the main population and any problems that may bring. Hopefully, we would continue with this trend.

On this journey we saw poverty, homeless on the streets and the devastation of this pandemic. It wasn't restricted to a small area; it was all over the world. We had seen it on the news regularly but to see it in person, it really shocked you. So many places were closed for good; shops, restaurants. The list just went on and on. It is hard to believe that we will bounce back from this. Life as we knew it will be changed… we have no choice.

Sunday 1st November
Left Cabuerniga, travelled through Cieza/Reinosa, Spain

It's a Spanish holiday today. They celebrate Todos Los Santos (All Saints' Day).

We got up at 6.30 a.m. We deliberately took Bruno on an extra-long walk as we decided to pack up and move on today. Breakfast all round, everything neatly stowed away, bill paid. We set off at 10 a.m. There were 588 miles left to Cadiz, eight and a half hours' travel time according to the satnav. We sail on the 10th November so it was 'steady as she goes'. We intended travelling an hour, resting, having refreshments, all stretching our legs and paws and giving the engine a rest from the inclines and descents. It was definitely hard work on the poor van.

10.53 a.m. Slight bang—van went into limp mode. I didn't know what that was. All I knew is the engine got louder and power was lost. We limped onto the hard shoulder on the bridge we were currently broken down on. Clive checked the engine and could see a hose off.

What a place to be stopped. Three lanes of fast-moving traffic on a huge bridge (no, not a bridge over troubled waters, although there could well be waterworks shortly). This was the one thing I had dreaded—breaking down in a foreign country; communication skills—zero.

11.15 a.m. European Breakdown cover was put into action. We were waiting for a young lady called Paris to ring back, which she promptly did. She advised Clive that two letters had been incorrectly documented on the system. NVG instead of NGV. The cover would therefore be invalid until we were able to contact the provider on Monday. Meanwhile, we would have to pay £400 to cover the costs of recovery. She sent Clive a link that provided her with our exact coordinates via satellite.

Shortly after we broke down, we saw a car a little way ahead of us pull up on the hard shoulder, I guess in the same situation as us, desperate.

12 o clock. Rescue called. They will text when they're en route.

No text was received; the next thing we knew, a Spanish guy turned up at 1 p.m. He had no intention of repairing the van. In fact, he didn't even look under the bonnet. He pulled up in front, approached us and told us??????? He spoke as much English as we did Spanish… zilch. Then, realising the language barrier, he used his phone to translate what he needed to say in very few words. He intended to tow us 25km to his base. He had to take the Nissan van then the caravan and explained that one would go with the van while the other stayed with the caravan. Clive told me to take Bruno with the van and he would wait with the caravan. Then an elderly Spanish couple emerged from the vehicle in front and had a very frantic conversation with our breakdown guy. I think he was going to send someone for them shortly. Well, that's a guess but I think that's what was said.

So, Bruno and I were in the front of the lorry with this man, the van on the back of his truck. I timed a 13-minute drive to their base. He offloaded the van and us and returned for Clive and the caravan.

2.39 p.m. Over an hour had passed from dropping me off. There was no sign of them returning and I had limited battery on my phone. A guy turned up at the yard over the road so I went to find out if he could tell me where Clive was. I wanted to know why he hadn't been returned to me. Via translation on my iPhone, I related the situation. He called someone and proceeded to tell me, in Spanish, and I can only assume by his expressions, that he would be on his way. No grasp of it at all. I felt a right dumbo.

I think the tow truck guy went back for the Spanish couple ahead of us as he would have returned with Clive hours ago. It was so frustrating. I really felt like sitting and blubbering but decided to have a stern conversation with myself. Blubbering won't help; it won't make everything right, so what's the point? Man up and get on with waiting, patiently, well, as patiently as I could muster and that is damned hard work for an impatient, over-excitable, volatile person like ME. After all, I told myself, Clive was in the same position as me, not knowing what was going on, blubbering? Of course, he wasn't. He'd be calm and collected, just whiling away the hours. Something I seemed to be greatly lacking in… Then the rescue company rang to say they needed payment of €216 per vehicle for the towing. Unbelievable.

By this time, Bruno and I had been there, in a lay-by opposite the breakdown yard, on an abandoned industrial estate, for an hour and a half. I spoke to Clive and he had heard nothing despite trying to call the tow company and breakdown services. By the time Clive saw the tow truck, we had been separated for two hours and forty minutes. I was in a real state. Bruno had been without a drink for 7 hours. I had no water in the Nissan van. It was all in the caravan. I felt terrible not having thought of that before leaving the caravan. I had nothing myself but that didn't really concern me; it was poor Bruno. Had I known beforehand that this was going to be a separation of hours, I would have been better prepared.

Clive got dropped off with me in the lay-by opposite their base. He was told he would be picked up at 9.30 a.m. to be towed to a mechanic. We had to pay the guy €321 in cash.

Hell of a day.

Luckily, we had plenty of food supplies and our water tanks had been topped up before we left El Molino de Cabuérniga that morning.

Monday 2nd November

We awoke at 7.30 a.m. Clive walked Bruno in readiness for collection at 9.30 by the Spanish man towing him to a mechanic. We had breakfast all round. Clive made some vital calls. It seemed the insurance company who sold us the breakdown cover had made several errors on the policy, firstly with the registration, then the European cover. It clearly stated on Clive's policy that we were covered but there was an issue arising from the insurance transferring to the rescue company. They said it didn't cover Europe and Clive's policy wasn't proof of cover. Really? What was the point of providing PDF's if not as documentary evidence? That was the lamest excuse EVER. The rescue company informed Clive that they would be taking it up with the insurance company, but, because of lockdown, this would take much longer. Meanwhile, in our own personal lockdown in a lay-by next to nowhere, having paid out €400 to the rescue company and €321 to the towing company, we were feeling rather perturbed and helpless. It was now 10.53 a.m. Clive had gone over the road to try and communicate with the towing company that our lift to the mechanic was well overdue. What was happening? We had supplies for three days tops and fresh water for that day. We had no mains electricity to charge our phones or anything else. We were at the mercy of the towing company. We were down to our last €200 cash. 10.55 a.m. The Spanish tow driver just surfaced beside the van, chatted fleetingly with a colleague then he was off. What next?

I couldn't turn my mobile on as I had less than 30% battery. My Fitbit was draining the life out of my mobile via the app on there. I had only just renewed my Fitbit because I had issues with the battery life. No improvement there. Grrrrr!

I couldn't help but feel very despondent. Clive said, 'It'll be alreet, Dolly' but I was far from being confident at the hands of this company. My journey from the bridge with this man was horrendous. We had the van on the back of his tow truck doing 90km/hr or more at times. The man was letting go of the steering wheel to use his mobile. At one point, the truck went into the next lane then towards the edge of the bridge. To my horror, the driver then started reaching around in the footwell and on the floor beside me. His eyes were not focused on the road at all at this point. He was looking for the remote which lowers the back of the truck. He had obviously misplaced it. He managed to retrieve it off the floor somewhere. I thought death was inevitable; I couldn't watch his antics, so I just squeezed Bruno into me as he was on my lap and wished the drive was over.

It was the worst drive of my life, literally. Then to wait nearly three hours for Clive to return to me with the caravan… It was awful.

Aaaah. Clive just appeared. He had talked to the tow company employees via good old iPhone translation. The nearest parts place was in Torrelavega. Not a clue where that was. We were probably looking at tomorrow for the part. Slight confusion somewhere. We were not being towed anywhere. They were organising the repair of our van so we had to stay put until the part arrived.

Clive was, as always, the optimist. Me, as always, the pessimist. UNTIL it happened, I'll not admit, accept, be a believer. As for Clive, in his eyes, it was already happening and on the way to being done………

I started this journey as a hopeful OPTIMIST. Two muppets abroad was slowly becoming 'Two disillusioned, sceptical, naïve muppets abroad, during a pandemic, that makes it 100 x worse!!!!!'

That 'Tow' Company…

Thank heavens Clive had emptied the toilet and filled up the water (not drinking) for showering and washing up. Luckily, Clive said he passed a garage on the way onto the industrial estate. I was oblivious on my journey here. I thought this man was not only a terrible driver but also a serial killer. All the way here I had myself dead and buried at his hands. Then, when he left me, telling me in a stern Spanish tone to 'stay here', I know he said that because he gestured with his arm pointing at the floor, I thought he was returning to kill me——The Australian film 'Wolf Creek' kept playing in my head. I'm convinced now that I am a loon—too much imagination. I had already lined up a magnificent array of weapons with which to maim my tormentor; several pencils, a corkscrew, some hacksaw blades. My dad had taught me well. Who knew he was just gonna leave us here to dehydrate, maybe eat one another——there it goes again. Maybe a psychiatrist will be introduced at some point to curb my overactive mad imagination. That or electric shock treatment. Although,

I think that boat sailed (my sanity) about the same time as the ferry from Harwich. No hope. Clive would probably concur at this point. I hadn't been the easiest of companions—he would say 'Doom and Gloom'.

He had been over with them for half an hour. I found five minutes hard going with Siri repeating my every word before turning it into Spanish. It was painfully longwinded.

I could see him wandering about with a guy. I hoped he was okay. It was very challenging being solely reliant on your iPhone as the one source of communication, especially when its battery was running out and, as yet, we had no source of recharging.

Bruno, bless him, was sleeping soundly. He calmed me with his nonchalant demeanour. If only I could have channelled that calm.

If Clive ever says, 'Calm, love', I lose it. It's like a red flag to a bull. A very angry, aggressive, noisy bull. In fact, I couldn't really think of any pleasant attributes at that moment. Why did he love me? I don't like me most of the time. Negativity personified. Impatient, volatile, voicing the OBVIOUS, (that annoys me yet I was bloody doing it myself)! I needed to slap myself. My Nan would say, 'If I had a third leg, I'd kick myself up the backside'. Well, she'd say 'ass'. I needed a lot of that myself at that present time… a third BIG leg.

Oooooh, 11.35 a.m. Clive returned, showed his face and said, 'We have action'. One sentence, then he was gone again.

11.48 a.m. Still not back. He is definitely a patient man—or defiantly patient. Not sure. Writing this down is helping though. Helping to show me my errors, faults, ridiculous mindset. I'll not change. In my head, I'm saying, 'I'll use this experience wisely and not be a negative force; I'll be more laid back', but, in reality, I'll do it again. I can't help myself. My big, fat MOOEY can't stop (big mouth)!

12.20 p.m. Still no Clive. What was he doing? Lots of comings and goings out of their yard but no sign of Clive since 11.35 a.m.

12.29 p.m. He was finally back. He informed me that the part was ordered and it would be in today (5 hours) and fixed today. Watch this space because I couldn't quite believe it.

3.49 p.m. Three men appeared beside our van. The part had just arrived. Clive said they are going to do it right now. WOW!

4.22 p.m. The van was repaired. It took 5 minutes to fit the new hose. They were now resetting the computer. That took longer than the repair. Unbelievable. Well, we had already paid out an ARM. I suspected this would be the LEG part of the transaction. The Spanish guy then took the van for a test drive.

The LEG was €329!!! That was very painful for a 5-minute repair and 10-minute computer reset.

We decided to bed in for the night as it had become too grey, wet, cold and uninviting to be setting off late in the day.

We walked Bruno, sorted out dinner for all, showered and retired to bed at 9 p.m. We would start afresh in the a.m…

Clive's bit:—*Oh dear, the turbo hose was blown off. The van went into limp mode which is designed to protect the engine. Never mind, I thought, we had got cover. It would be maybe a day's delay. But it seemed that someone had made an error. I know Lisa has covered it anyway. They turned up and took Lisa and Bruno away. The lorries, as they thundered past, moved out to the middle lane, but the caravan still shook. The cars flew by fast. I sat and watched the horses in the field beside me and the traffic on the road. Lisa sent me a text so I knew she was okay. The minutes became hours as the time slowly ticked away. We texted each other, I called the breakdown, I was going nowhere fast. I didn't despair, I knew it would be 'alreet' (smiled to myself). Then, hours later (a day at least!), the guy turned up and we were off, at speed too. Eventually, I was back with them (hugs). I put the caravan back on the van, put the legs down and got a cup of tea made.*

It's fine, dolly…………

The next day, I must have been a right pain for these mechanics trying to get things sorted. I needed to know we were going to be sorted out and away, so through Google translate (thank you), they got the process moving. Next day (oh my), yes, yes, yes, the part was there and they were doing it. In next to no time, it was all done. The hose had to be a 'genuine' part and boy, that cost us.

Tuesday 3rd November
Leaving Reinosa, Spain. Travelled through Coria del Rio

330 miles to go, 4 hours of travel. We booked in for Friday 6th until 10th at La Rosaleda Camping, Conil de la Frontera, Cadiz. It was a little off-track but we had plenty of time for a few days' stopover. Cadiz was where the ferry departed from and took us to Tenerife. I could actually see a light at the end of the tunnel now.

Up at 5 a.m. Walkies, brekkie, packed up and we were off. It was 8 a.m. and we were finally saying 'ADIOS' to the tow/breakdown at Reinosa.

We were now on the A67 once more. Steady as she blows. Another long road, no checking road signs for quite some time.

9.18 a.m. This was our first stop for toilets and a quick walk for Bruno. It was colder today and bleak. We were hopeful it would improve with time.

And it did—the sun appeared as everything else darkened, mainly our moods because Clive decided to go slightly off-piste to a caravan camping site that was open, APPARENTLY, according to his iPhone app. There was no answer on the phone which, to me, is a bad sign. We went there via a busy town, ramps with numerous varying degrees of head-banging and a caravan jumping and bouncing more and more as firstly my mood darkened, then his. We arrived to find a SHUT sign. Who'd have thunked it? Me is who.

200 miles of travelling and we had finally come across a Mercadona; great. But NO. When your van is over 4 metres long and your caravan is 6.4 metres—parking spaces along a busy high street were not going to accommodate these two. You can't just unhook your caravan somewhere and go off in the van. Together as a unit you're fairly invincible. Separated, you're vulnerable. So, we had to pass the invitation of the large supermarket and, yep, plump for another Lidl for they have a more voluptuous car park. This was unfortunate in the case of lack of choice compared to the UK, but fortunate if you're in dire need.

Since driving into Spain, the parking areas had become sparse. In France, whenever there was a petrol station, there soon followed large parking areas for lorries, caravans and cars. In Spain, we struggled to find anything suitable, even a scrap of land or lay-by. There had been plenty of petrol stations but very few parking spaces, and those that were there had been taken up already with lorries. We were going to stop regularly to give the engine a break but this was proving more difficult than we anticipated because of the lack of ample parking facilities. As I said earlier, we needed a rather long space to house the Nissan van and the caravan together.

After Lidl, we got back on the dual carriageway searching for parking for the night which we eventually found at 4.30 p.m. This required some skill as it was on a slope and the caravan hand brake was insufficient to stop it creeping forward. A bit of a tyre wedge and legs firmly down, everything levelled and we were set. Things were looking reasonable apart from our moods.

We were surrounded by beautiful wooded areas that looked perfect for walking Bruno then I saw a huge boxer dog roaming around alone. No late walkies off-lead for us.

It ended up being a late one talking out our anger issues. Nearly 12 o'clock. Ok, there were a lot of issues and someone, not me, of course, had an apology for spitting out his dummy. He had every right to let off steam since he had suffered at the hands of idiot drivers and incorrect satnav directions which had led us into unknown territory with regards to excruciatingly small roads which felt more like narrow paths trying to squeeze through with the beast. That's what the van and caravan became once hooked together. One trip took us over a very slender (one vehicle wide) bridge which ended up being the wrong road. On our return, the bridge had been taken over by numerous workmen like ants on a sugary bun, who waved us to go back. We had to go back the wrong way again. We were the first in a long line of traffic so we had to wait for the queue to disperse before we could move. It was then our turn to reverse, but not in the conventional way. There was no room to manoeuvre the caravan. Plus, it would have turned into another 50-point turn. Inexperience is a huge negative in this field. We had to take the caravan off the van and manually reverse it with the kind help of one of the Spanish workmen, then hook it back up to the towing hitch. Once we were on the move again, we had to find an alternative route to make our way back in the right direction. That added on a big chunk of time and frustration.

By then, Clive had simply had enough of the stress and some muppet, namely me, nagging on. Well, I was paranoid about him breaking the van. I know it wasn't his fault but I worry. He had a bit of a tantrum, then a lot of miles to mull things over because it was VERY, VERY QUIET. Hmmmmmm…

So, after long talks, laughter and some name-calling, we eventually slept……

Wednesday 4th November

Up at 7.20 a.m. The usual walkies and breakfast.

9.15 a.m. We checked on our mobiles for the nearest shop. As soon as we located something along our intended route, we hit directions and set off to drive to the Lupa shop Google had found. We got our essentials, made a decision on spag bol for dinner and left the shop at 9.45 a.m. We stopped after an hour's travelling as soon as we saw parking as we had no idea when the next one would be.

3.23 hours left, 227 miles.

We had a toilet break, tea and biscuits and a walk around the perimeter of the petrol station for Bruno. We set off soon after but decided we should take things fairly easy as there were still extremes of inclines and descents so we didn't want anything going awry.

2.20 p.m. As soon as we came across services from then on, we quickly took advantage. So, when we came across the CEPSA gas station with a huge area of rough ground to park on, we decided to call it a day. It was well lit so we parked up behind the petrol station building and a picnic area. They had an outside tap to refill our water and a small shop for any other essentials we might need. We showered (bucket and jug style), had dinner and were in bed by 10 p.m. It rained all night but I quite like the soothing sound of the rainfall on the metal of a caravan roof; its melody is hypnotic, calming and sleep-inducing.

Thursday 5th November
Conil de la Frontera, Spain

We slept like logs and awoke at 6 a.m. to muddy puddles. The early walk wasn't too pleasant but essential for someone to have their constitutionals and as soon as he did, we wound up the caravan legs and set off by 7.50 a.m… well, after breakfast and several cups of tea. It's obligatory for us Brits, isn't it? I need at least one strong morning cuppa if not two.

We stopped at 9 a.m. for diesel, toilet breaks and a brew. We then travelled on at a casual speed. We stopped again at 10 a.m. for some brunch as we had bought fresh baguettes, serrano ham, cheese, tomatoes and onions. I enjoyed the tea breaks and outgoings with Bruno at the services. It was nice to walk around in the caravan and stretch your legs after being stuck in the van then get out into the fresh air even if it was only to have a 20-minute walk around petrol stations. They have been, for the most part, very pretty and well-kept considering the number of people that pass through them.

The caravan cooker had been a godsend too. It performed exceptionally well. We had fresh food every day. Both Clive and I love to cook so we do most things together.

Even though the caravan was compact in the kitchen area, there was a pull-out worktop which Clive used and workspace by the cooker and under the cupboard beside the door for me. We worked well together in the kitchen. I really enjoyed the whole caravanning experience.

It was wet and windy so we decided to have a leisurely drive. We had until midday the following day to arrive at the caravan park so there was no rush.

We were 1738 feet above sea level there which made our ears pop. The scenery was phenomenal. The mountainous views were spectacular.

147 miles left and 2.18 hours left.

12.44 p.m. We were almost at our destination. Making our way to the caravan site right near the ferry terminal, we seemed to be chasing the sun. It started off chilly, and then we had windows right down, enjoying the breeze.

It would be our last stop that night before we had a few days' break from driving. We found a lorry park to settle into for the night. There weren't many miles left to travel for the morning so we decided to have a nice dinner of sausages, mash, onion gravy and peas, glass of wine, watch a film, shower and relax in bed. We were both relieved and amazed to be there.

Friday 6th November

We got up at 7 a.m., had a long walk and a casual, relaxed breakfast since there was no rush. We got packed and were off by 9 a.m. We were now only a couple of hours from Camping La Rosaleda. It was a gorgeous day and my mood had improved enormously (thankfully) knowing that we would soon be a stone's throw from our ferry ride to Tenerife. The Port at Cadiz was a short journey from Conil. Brilliant.

We arrived at Conil de la Frontera at lunchtime, booked in at reception and were given a sheet of plots to choose from as it was almost bereft of visitors. We drove around looking for the perfect spot to reverse onto, a level piece of ground with easy access.

After a couple of attempts at reversing, Clive decided to detach the caravan from the towing hitch and use the motor mover. What an amazing piece of kit! It made the job so quick and worked perfectly. We were both well impressed.

We got ourselves comfortable, had a good look around the site, checked out all the amenities, then finally, excursions without the caravan in tow, which was so much easier, believe me. The joy of being able to park anywhere without worry. Not having to contend with small roads whilst having a nervous breakdown thinking how the hell were we going to manoeuvre through there or round that sharp bend? The relief was most welcome.

Clive's bit:—*The drive there was pretty much uneventful. The roads were not as good as in France but the scenery was spectacular. The caravan park and its facilities were phenomenal. The electric hook up allowed us to charge everything and get a good rest in.*

Bruno ran around the beach excitedly like a spring lamb. He loved the space and freedom and paddled his feet in the clear blue water.

We were really going to enjoy this break and the area needed some serious exploring over the next few days, especially as we were free—no towing the beast.

We would now be able to explore more shops. Mercadona was first for a much better selection of groceries.

On the way back onto the site, we stopped so I could purchase tokens for the washing machine and dryer. I did bring a length of washing line which we could hang on the trees on our plot but it wasn't long enough to dry everything. Wash load 1 was completed. I decided to do more the next day; after all, we had until the 10th so there was no immediate rush.

We had a lovely relaxed evening, watched a film after dinner and had a glass of wine before a steamy hot power shower then bed. It was bliss. Mains power, sunny days, warm weather to dry washing, beautiful picturesque area that was so quiet, peaceful and tranquil and more days in which to be properly spoilt. We were so lucky to have the extra time on the journey which made it an extended holiday. Things were obviously closed because of the pandemic which meant there wasn't much to do in the way of restaurants, parks and the usual things people do on holiday, but not taking into account the breakdown, we had a really enjoyable trip. We don't really do restaurants or excursions often, even on holiday. We are both homebodies, enjoying cooking and watching movies on Netflix; it's a simple lifestyle but we are at ease with it.

Saturday 7th November

Our body alarm clocks still seem to be stuck at 7 a.m., so we were up and out with Bruno on a lovely long walk around the site exploring. We met a couple who lived in a motor home there all year round. We chatted to them about our destination amongst other pleasantries.

Back to the caravan for breakfast. Wash load numbers two and three. I ruined the lovely fake fur blanket I used to throw on our leather sofa at home and Bruno's fleecy blanky by melting them in the hot tumble dryer. They were only brought as extra throws for warmth and they were becoming redundant anyway—that excused me for stupidly destroying them. Bin job for those, unfortunately. We then set off to Mercadona before going to the beach for another long walk. The weather was so warm and sunny and the beach was glorious. There were no restrictions walking Bruno there so, whenever possible, we took long walks on the soft, warm golden sand at the water's edge. It was lovely to paddle and cool a little in the heat of the sun.

Sunday 8th November

We were much more relaxed and started to lie in better knowing we didn't have to shoot off on the motorway.

It was pleasant getting up at our own speed, taking Bruno out in the warm, dry weather, and having a chat with the few people that lived there on our morning walk. A couple just across from our plot were driving a motor home. They were going off to Portugal to live. They had to stop over here for a few weeks as they had set off without having shut their roof vent so it had been ripped off leaving them vulnerable to the elements. They had to order a new one from England and wait for its arrival. This too had been their virgin journey in a motor home. So, it turned out we were not the only dingbats embarking on a life-changing venture being ill-prepared for the experience; Ill-prepared with regard to the working parts on the caravan, water heater and shower namely. We all had a good laugh at our comedic incidents. They were now repaired and ready to go so we wished them well as they did us.

We had a lazy evening meal, pasta and homemade garlic bread and wine. I had a very enjoyable shower with a sweet gecko overhead as my only companion in the whole shower block, then we were off to bed.

Monday 9th November

Day 2 of a sleep-in. We seemed to be finally relaxing as we didn't wake until 8 a.m. Bruno too was enjoying spreading out on our bed with his other soft fleecy blanket. We literally had to nudge him off the bed to get him out in the mornings. Because it was virtually empty on-site, we were able to leave Bruno off-lead when we strolled around, which he loved. He didn't stray far, he was just nosy and checked out most bays, sniffing around and doing his doggy things.

I used up my last tokens on our final wash load. So, everything was washed, dried, ironed and we were totally ready for off the next day.

We popped back to the beach for a long walk before a grocery shop and lunch.

We really enjoyed our stay there. It was off the beaten track on this site but only a 10-minute drive to the shops so you had the best of both worlds. The site was immaculate and tidy. They had all the mod cons. Everything you needed. I would definitely go back to both the sites we stopped at.

Tuesday 10th November
Leaving day… We travelled to Cadiz port through Andalusia and Seville

We got up early, walked Bruno, had breakfast and had started packing up when a guy turned up. It was the couple we had met who lived there in their motor home. He deliberately came looking for us. He thought we'd set off yesterday. He said his wife had walked round the day before and couldn't find us so they thought we'd left earlier than planned to avoid the lockdown which had gone into effect the night before. He said it was all over the news. We told him we didn't have a TV. They didn't either, apparently; his wife had seen it on her computer. He was concerned we wouldn't make it to the ferry. We bid the guy farewell and told him we didn't want to see him again, in the nicest possible way, of course; we did want to get our ferry after all.

I was panicking but Clive was fine. I thought the ferry might be cancelled.

We made our way to Cadiz thinking we might be stopped. We arrived at noon. Clive went and booked us in. Everything was fine. No problem at all, to my amazement.

We put the legs down on the caravan. I made pasta for lunch. I threw everything that needed to be used up into the concoction—bacon, prosciutto, ham, onion, peppers, cream cheese, white wine, grated cheese on top. It was so tasty. I then made up ham, cheese and tomato baguettes for the evening on the ferry because we weren't sure what would be open on there.

2 p.m. We were moved into the next parking area in the order of places where we would be leaving the ferry, i.e., Arrecife, Las Palmas then us, Santa Cruz so that exiting would be easy.

Clive was asked to reverse into a long parking space. Yikes, reversing—still not too experienced with that task. He managed some way then unhooked the van and manually moved it into place just to get the job sorted quickly as it was very busy.

3 p.m. We were moved onto the ferry and expertly manoeuvred into place by a very patient Spanish guy who was proficient at hand-signalling the wheel directions to get the van and caravan reversed into a very tight, well-packed parking bay.

When we checked in, we were given meal vouchers for the whole trip. That was a nice surprise because we had no idea this was in with the price of the ferry booking. The vouchers included breakfast, lunch and dinner plus drinks. We asked if we could book a cabin but were told we had to wait until we sailed.

We took Bruno to the pet area and locked him in his cage with his bed, blankets and dishes.

We sailed at 4.15 p.m. and waited near reception once we left port. Before we knew it, the lady from check-in came to get us from the waiting area so we could book a cabin. Clive paid €148 instead of the pre-booking price of €340. Bargain. There were two single beds, a shower, toilet, towels and bedding. Excellent. Lovely hot shower and the room was everything you needed—clean, cool and spacious.

We went to see Bruno almost every hour to walk him and make a fuss of him. He really didn't like the cage but we had no choice.

Wednesday 11th November

We got up early (6 a.m.) to walk and feed Bruno. It wasn't much of a walk around the deck but we did the circumference several times so he could relieve himself. We then had to wait for the restaurant to open so we lay on our beds playing games on the iPhone. We paid for the internet as there was little else to do once you were in your cabin.

We went to the restaurant for a hot drink, namely a bucket of tea, please. Nope. The clocks had changed the night before. 7.30 a.m. was now 6.30 a.m., so back off to see Bruno. After a patient wait, we went back for opening.

Breakfast—Clive had scrambled eggs, bacon, frankfurter sausages and toast and a bottle of water. I had scrambled eggs on toast. We had to wait for coffee as no hot drinks came with breakfast.

Lunch—Fish and chips with rice for me and Clive had pasta with his. Strange combo.

Dinner—I had chicken and chips and Clive had lasagne, fish and chips. None of the food was piping hot but it was excellent quality and most enjoyable.

Thursday 12th November

Clive woke at 5 a.m. as he said we were arriving at Tenerife. We were up and packed, then saw Bruno for his walk. It was then we realised we were only just leaving Las Palmas. Santa Cruz was our next stop at about 8.20 a.m. Grrrrrrr!

We had no meal vouchers left at this point but we had cash to pay. I chose toast and a Spanish torte slice. Clive had scrambled eggs, frankfurters, toast and finally, two cafés con leche. We got money out to pay and the guy on the till said "No", it was in with the trip. That was a pleasant surprise.

Before today, the option of a hot drink had not been available, just juice or water, and I don't actually function properly without my cup of tea or continental coffee. Now, hot beverages galore…

We went back to walk and feed Bruno then went down to our deck to get ready to leave.

We left the ferry swiftly and exited the port then made our way to Golf del Sur. We arrived at 10 a.m. at

Clive's parents' place (Marlene is his mum and David, his dad). We went in for coffee before they showed us to our apartment which we had rented in advance. Clive organised it through a friend of his mum's and they had been given the keys in readiness for our arrival. We had to negotiate a mini roundabout to turn around outside the apartment block. Unfortunately, the caravan was too long to make it. We had a small incident where the caravan hit the stone roundabout and got a nasty dent. Clive had to release it from the van's tow bar and move it manually into its parking space along the road outside.

We started on the job of unpacking the caravan but had to stop to walk Bruno to Clive's mum's for our lunch invitation. She had prepared a ham salad, potato torte, fresh baguettes and avocado. Yum. She is an excellent hostess and cook. We always get spoilt by them. After a most enjoyable visit, we walked back home. Bruno was shattered so we continued unpacking the caravan and left him to snooze. Clive's mum and dad had invited us back for an evening meal so we drove this time. We had chilli, rice, Doritos and dips which was very well received. After dinner, we had sundowners in the garden overlooking the golf course and the ocean, which is a beautiful sight. The evening was most enjoyable. As we were leaving about 9.30 p.m., Clive's mum told us her friend had offered to let us put the caravan on her property so we made arrangements to go there the next day.

We got home, gave Bruno a quick walk, had a shower, glass of vino then bed, as all three of us were absolutely shattered. With the excitement of arriving and the ferry journey, although very pleasant and calm, neither of us had slept well because we knew Bruno was imprisoned which made it hard to relax when he was in your every thought.

Friday 13th November

Clive was up at 6, me at 7. We walked Bruno and finished unpacking the caravan.

We were picked up at 9.30 a.m. by David to go off and meet Marlene and her friends for brunch as they had been to the gym for a yoga lesson.

We had coffee and a mixto toasty, ham and cheese. David dropped us off after showing us where Rachel lived so we could drop the caravan round there later.

We came back, hooked the caravan onto the tow bar and drove to Rachel's. She had opened the gates ready for us. The slope leading onto her enclosed property was very steep. We had to align the caravan manually facing the drive as the area was too narrow to do it attached to the van. It was then put on the tow bar and Clive carefully made his way up the drive. The first attempt failed so he tried again a bit faster and with more power. One of the caravan feet caught on the kerb edge and got completely bent out of shape but he was in. A pattern seemed to be emerging; another limp. There was also a strong smell of burnt rubber from the tyres gripping the tiled entrance as he gave it some welly. I thought the clutch was broken but Clive thought it was the tyres slipping on the tiled slope.

VERY STRESSFUL

Good foot……… Limp foot………

We unhooked the caravan and used the motor mover to position it away from the drive with the hope that there would be one more move to our forever home.

We went shopping after then later met with Clive's parents for drinks. We all went for Chinese at their favourite restaurant just down the road from our apartment. The food there was fantastic and the service impeccable as always. We had our fill of food and wine, said our good nights and then walked home.

I think we were beginning to finally let our hair down that day as we relaxed into the afternoon and sank a few bevvies at dinner. Clive drank a little too much. He said his feet were killing him on the way back so he sat on the kerb edge, whining.

The walk is very short, 5 minutes at best. I, being gentle and kind, told him to man up and get home. Sweet is my middle name, NOT.

Saturday 14th November

I woke early, around 6ish, made some tea and decided to walk Bruno alone, as he was a bit lacklustre after the night before. I had a lovely stroll which kept me out for 40 minutes. It is very much like Cornwall here, rolling hills and undulating coastal walks. We had walked the legs off Bruno and ourselves trying to make up for the hours of travelling and being cooped up. We were now walking over 8 miles a day. Today, my stomach was sore, abdomen, calf muscles, most places, really. In fact, we both looked like we'd had an unfortunate accident, one you don't want to admit to, walking strangely. We had backaches. This healthy lifestyle is gruelling, arduous, violent and anything else which describes our distasteful postures.

We were settling in better and getting used to the apartment life.

Sunday 15th November

We got up at 7 a.m. Usual routine of walking Bruno before breakfast and organising the busy (not) day.

We walked 5 minutes up the road to the Hiperdino and bought fillet steak, salad and jacket spuds for dinner.

We had a fairly uneventful day apart from 8 miles of walking but there were no complaints about the beautiful weather and the breathtaking scenery.

Monday 16th November

Clive's mum sent a link about "Age in Spain". It's a charity organisation put in place to help you become a resident on the island. Clive found a pop-up help desk down the road at the Winter Gardens so we decided to go there after our morning walk.

We drove to the area, parked up and started to look for the help desk. We walked round and round, not having much luck so we waited to go in the Bowl's Club reception area once it became vacant (COVID restrictions). Then Clive spotted a table outside next door to the Bowl's Club with an A4 noticeboard saying "Age in Spain".

Brilliant.

We walked over as the couple sitting at the desk got up to leave so we were able to sit straight down and speak to the lady about residency. She was very informative and pleasant. We need:—

- NIE
- Get Spanish Bank Accounts
- Private Health Insurance

- Rental Contract for our apartment
- Autonomo for Clive (self-employed paperwork)
- Have €4,500 each in the bank.

She very kindly made us an appointment with the Padron for 8.30 a.m. Friday 27th November at the SAC (council offices), Las Chafiras to start the process for our NIE paperwork. An NIE is required to open a Spanish bank account. Then, before the end of December this year, we would have to be in the system here in order to apply for TIE cards to stay in Tenerife. Residency for TIE is a long process demanding its own set of requirements. It's an identification card the size of your plastic driving licence, containing your picture and all your information. We also need to organise new Spanish mobile numbers. We need this to open our bank account and for residency, i.e., TIE paperwork.

5.30 p.m. We met with Clive's mum and dad at the 19th Hole (a very pleasant bar/restaurant). We were only supposed to be having a couple of drinks but ended up staying and having pizzas all round, such was our enjoyment. We left about 9 p.m. to walk home.

It still felt like an extended holiday. I was still trying to get my head around the fact that we were here, here for good. Wow. We had really got here. I didn't think we would make it after escaping so many lockdowns on our journey. We had seen police stopping travellers, roadblocks and other COVID restrictions. It was a miracle really.

Tuesday 17th November

We rose about 7.45 a.m. Walked Bruno in the beautiful, warm, sunny weather. It seemed so weird going out in shorts and vests in November. The weather forecasts for England were so gloomy and depressing. It wasn't that long ago we were in the thick of it; rain, blustery winds, snow. It was hard to comprehend the extremes in such a short period of time.

We had to go out to source new ink cartridges for our HP printer. Worten here is similar to Curry's, just a bit more expensive but, as Clive kept telling me, everything has to be shipped or flown in adding further expense. Hmmmm…

It is imperative that you have a working printer as everything you do requires a form or photocopy to be printed out.

We ended up leaving the shop with a Freesat tv box plus ink cartridges. When we got home, we couldn't fit the box as we needed more cables. We popped into China Town (it's a huge Chinese shop selling virtually everything). We bought cables, printer paper, writing material but we still needed another cable. The English channels we have on our tv are very limited. After having Sky in the UK, hundreds of channels at your disposal, then being reduced to terrestrial tv, it's a bit of a shock to the system. You don't realise how over-indulged you've been with the basics, well, what you think are basics, until you only have 5 channels to choose from. No pause or rewind! Tea and toilet intermissions no more!! Shocking.

Oh, we were like spoilt children, having their iPhones surgically removed.

We had been listening to Coast Radio whilst driving around. It's an English station with lots of adverts about residency requirements, mobile phone companies and other various companies which help you if you want to move/live here. One such advert was for a company called Lobster whose mobile phone prices seemed very reasonable compared to some here that are more commonly used. Clive rang them and tried to organise for us to get new SIM cards. We cannot do this without first obtaining our NIE numbers but we have been advised that we need Spanish mobile numbers in order to obtain our NIEs. It was very frustrating.

Wednesday 18th November

Clive was up before me so left me to have a sleep in while he walked Bruno. We had breakfast then went out to Iceland (Overseas Iceland), then Mercadona. Iceland, let me tell you, is nothing like the UK Iceland. They have a lot of the same stock which still has the UK price labels on but when you look at the shelf edge for the price, hmmmm, add at least €2 on. A block of cheese says £2.00 but when you check the real price, it is actually €4.50. Yes, more than double for most of the items. A box of teabags—€9.50. It is an expensive pastime getting anything in there. A gentleman in front of me in the queue put a couple of items on the conveyor, and, when the girl said €8.50, he recoiled slightly. He then pointed out that his two items had labels on which added up to £3.50, to which the girl explained that was the UK price, not the price here. He ended up leaving without his two items. It did make me grin. If you have been here a while and have a longing for a particular English dish, then, believe me, you will indulge yourself and pay the extra. I always laugh at the English queuing up for the usual greasy spoon breakfast whilst abroad. Why the hell would you want to travel 3,000 miles to a hot destination just to search out and relive your English breakfast/lunch/dinner? I don't get it. But wait, after 4 or 6 months, I longed for a pork pie or Sunday roast. Such was the craving that we embarked on our own challenge. Yup, hot water pastry, the perfect jelly around the pork filling. The Iceland frozen pork pies just did not hit the mark. Our pastry, well, the whole kit and caboodle, was absolutely delicious, one that we will be revisiting very soon. We embrace most things Spanish but do miss the oddest things at times. Mine is jumping in my Micra, shooting to Morrison's/Asda/Tesco, picking up new underwear, a summer top or shorts, maybe a leaf blower, I don't know, things that you just can't pick up off the shelf here. Not being able to do that grates, but then, I awake to the sun EVERY day. Glorious sunshine, scenery you dream of on those dull, wet, windy, blustery days, with hailstones and high winds—I'd add frosty but I did enjoy a walk on a frosty morning—but in the most part, I prefer it here. The pros and cons are heavily weighted on the pros!

After Iceland, we popped into the Home Shop for some silicone tongs. Nope, no one seems to stock them, only metal ones which I refuse to use on any of my pans. A trip will be required to Ikea. They have a very small one in Las Chafiras. The normal-sized one lies in Santa Cruz. If I can't find what I need here then Santa Cruz will be next on the list.

When we got home, Marlene rang to see if we were home and they popped in for a coffee to see how we were doing. We chatted about the things we need to get for residency.

They are taking us to their car mechanic in the morning as his daughter knows everything about transferring our driving licences over, car insurance, house insurance, most things really. She went through the education system here so is fluent in Spanish.

Marlene said she would come with us next Friday 27th to the SAC office to translate as she is proficient in Spanish, having attended several College courses. It certainly makes you feel like a dumbo having no communication skills. We should have learnt the basics at least. Shame on us!

Thursday 19th November

We followed Marlene and David to their mechanic's shop and went in to see the very helpful young lady in reception. She has a wealth of knowledge having grown up here.

The Great Brexit Exit

Clive's work van—Gutted; he can't keep it as Brexit means there's no agreement for these things now. If it's not gone by 31st December or taken back to England, it will be impounded and crushed. ☹

We have to expedite our NIE applications which then gives us 6 months to transfer our driving licences after Brexit.

We left there very despondent about Clive's van but with a long list of things we need to do and a whole lot of useful information we needed to know.

After lunch, we went back to the mechanic's to source more information about TIE requirements as I hadn't asked everything I wanted, and, now we knew how to get there, it was on our to-do list.

We went to reception and the young lady spoke to Clive about his van as she knew someone who might be interested in buying it. He agreed for her to set up a meet which was arranged for 3.30 p.m. the same day.

We talked about other options available to us. Driving it back to England to sell involved two ferries at a large cost, tolls through France, diesel, a long drive, accommodation during travel and the risk of lockdown or isolating because of COVID.

Marlene suggested sending it by container. Great idea. Clive rang the container company. No. Because it wasn't imported, it cannot be exported. Aaaaaah.☹☹

We were given a link for the NIE applications so I emailed them at 1.22 p.m. and got a reply at 1.45 p.m. with an appointment the very next day at 10.15 a.m. at the Policia Nacional which is the local police. Wow, we were told the wait for an appointment was lengthy so this was a big surprise. We needed our rental contract which we did not have. We had to download form Tasa 790 to complete and take with our passports. Tasa 790 had to be taken to the bank to pay the tax (roughly €9.00), plus passport photos.

3.30 p.m. That painful meeting. Not our favourite to date. Clive had his van for three years, and having paid £10,000, he was now being offered €1,200. This guy had to pay a driver €1,500 to take it back to the UK. Clive begrudgingly accepted the offer. Now he had to look for a people carrier with privacy windows as the only vans allowed here were owned by companies. We were shown a Citroen C4 Picasso with privacy windows, about 12 years old, €5,500. So, the €1,200 went straight down on the C4 as a deposit. I felt like crying; I loved his van. We had no other choice really. We went back and sold the van.

We left and walked onto Centro de Reconocimiento de Conductores in Las Chafiras in order to obtain photographs for our appointment tomorrow. We had a 45-minute wait outside before eventually getting our small envelopes with four passport-sized photos. (€10).

Having become carless and not knowing where to find a taxi to get home, we walked the 35-minute power walk, total steps for the day 23,272, equating to 9.68 miles, burnt 2,487 calories. We got home just after 7 p.m. Walked Bruno, nuked a lasagne then embarked on the task of downloading Tasa 790 to complete. Our HP printer would not connect to the internet so we couldn't print the form. Marlene rang and Clive explained the problem. She came round with her laptop and connected via cable to our printer.

She completed the forms online for us and printed them off. Yayyyyy! She said David would collect us at 8.30 a.m. then drop us in Las Chafiras to go to the bank to pay for the forms.

Friday 20th November

We queued at Santander and eventually got in only to be told they couldn't do it there. They told us to go to B.B.V.A. which is in another town. We came out of there and went into Sabadell right next door. Clive said it was worth a try as we had to get to our 10.15 a.m. appointment. We queued again. By this time, it was 9 a.m. Clive had to go in alone (COVID). He messaged me to go in to sign forms. I was let in by the teller, signed forms, returned outside and waited. Clive came out with the paid printed forms. He messaged our friend Sara to find out which was our local Policia. She said we had to go to Las Americas. We found a taxi rank, jumped in a taxi and made our way to the Policia Nacional. The driver understood us immediately, thank goodness.

€18.00 taxi journey right outside the official building. We were 25 minutes early. Clive showed an officer our paperwork and he motioned for us to go inside. The officer jokingly called us Bonnie and Clyde as Clive is pronounced very differently in Spanish, more like Clyde.

Clive was led to a female officer and me, a man. We handed over our forms, passports, rental agreement and photographs. The rental agreement and photos were not required. Photocopies of passports were. The policeman moaned at me in Spanish, threw my paperwork in front of me on the desk then sent me away. He got up and moved away from his desk leaving me flummoxed and feeling stupid. The female officer dealing with Clive handed him two forms to complete, one for each of us, and told him to get copies of our passports at a shop over the road. So, he took on the task of completing our forms and sent me off to get photocopies. I accepted the challenge even though I didn't have a clue how to say photocopy or Spanish numbers or where the hell the shop was. I googled photocopy shop, photocopies and two. As it happens and it seems to be the case across Spain, where there is a police station, there is ALWAYS a photocopy shop over the road. They are synonymous. Anywho, I crossed a couple of roads to a row of shops and lo and behold, Tienda de Fotocopias. Two is dos. Handed over the passports, dos fotocopias. 80 cents. Done. I headed back to the Policia, went up the wrong ramp, got told off and sent back. Dumbo.

When I found Clive, he was still translating the form so he could fill it in. When he finished, we went back to the now-empty help desk area. We stood and waited. Be prepared to wait a loooong time. The guy who moaned me away walked by us several times glaring at me; I could feel his distaste.

The female officer once again called Clive, she questioned him about not having a Spanish mobile number and luckily accepted that this was in fact in motion, so she gave him his form to check and told him to go and SIT, more of a command really.

She waited some time before she called out Lisa; my turn. I gave her my papers then had to go sit and wait with Clive. It didn't take her long to recall me to check my form. We both confirmed everything was correct so we thanked her and left.

After a lengthy walk, we found a taxi to get back home. On returning, we hired a car for a week, then drove home for lunch as we'd had to rush out before we had a chance for any breakfast in the morning. It was a mad dash but worth it as we were now in possession of our official NIE numbers.

It was now appointment time for our health insurance. A Spanish guy came to our apartment to complete the relevant forms. We had to pay him €100 commission. He said he would be in touch with the documents shortly.

Another job jobbed.

Clive then rang Lobster to order and pay for our new SIM cards. They would be posted to us. At least once we had those and our new Spanish numbers, we would be able to log that information on our TIE paperwork.

We went out in our little Panda hire car. It was my first drive here on the wrong side of the road. Well, for me. it's wrong. It's strange going round roundabouts in the opposite direction. It doesn't take you long to adapt. Las Chafiras though—nightmare. The main drag has roads crossing it regularly and one road will be one-way traffic, the next, both directions are coming at you, then the next from the other way. Drivers here do not use their indicators. It's bizarre and frightening. I'm not fond of it, to be honest.

After that drive, Clive said there were teeth marks in the dashboard but he fibs.

Next on the list, Spanish bank accounts. First thing on the list for Monday. Driving licences were now in the system to be transferred. As soon as we could get confirmation of TIE, they can be finalised. At least now we had 6 months' grace.

Saturday 21st November

Up before 7 a.m., walked Bruno and had breakfast.

11 a.m. Champagne brunch at M's for Clive's mum's belated birthday gift. I drove to El Medano, where we all had brunch. After dropping Marlene and David back home, we went to Adeje, Lidl, Koala pet shop then Mercadona. We certainly lead an interesting life. We are getting to grips with all the various outlets. It's unlike the UK in that you just can't go to one supermarket and pick up all the things you are used to. Mercadona sells food and cleaning products. You cannot buy crockery, clothes, shoes, car oil, light bulbs, and the list goes on. You have to go to specific shops for specific items. And, this will shock a lot of people—it's old school, the big shops shut on Sundays. Yep, it's a shock to the system but we survive.

I think it's a good thing really. It is still a day of rest here. You will find small shops open and in the densely populated holiday resort areas, there will always be a Hiperdino or small shop open.

In the afternoon, we popped into Marlene and Dave's for a cuppa and catch up, then home and out with Bruno for walkies.

For dinner, we had a Mercadona Catherine wheel sausage which is very tasty so we had that with new potatoes and peas. There are always leftovers for lunch the next day.

Mercadona produce is excellent. Lamb doesn't seem to be very popular which is unfortunate because it is my favourite meat. They do small lamb chops and legs of lamb but they are very small and expensive by comparison, and I am a very big meat-eater so fat lamb chops are preferable.

Sunday 22nd November

We were up early, before 7 a.m., had a quick cuppa and then off out for Bruno's morning walk then back for breakfast which, unlike our normal quick bowl of cereals or toast, now includes clusters of cereals with nuts, natural Greek yoghurt and the occasional fresh fruit which is glorious. I always thought it was rubbish when I heard people say 'fruit and vegetables abroad are better in flavour and juicier'. It's true, they are soooo tasty. I can't believe how my tastebuds have come alive. I really don't like avocado in the UK. It is bland and just not desirable.

Here, different story. They have buckets of flavour, soft, yielding, juicy and absolutely delicious. Clive's mum uses them regularly and has got me hooked on them now.

2 p.m. We drove to Marlene and Dave's then all went to their recommended eatery, Servelyn's at Calle Canada Blanca, Parque la Reina. Clive's mum recommended a dish which we both ended up having, namely, garlic chicken, potato and mushroom, which was splendid. We had to get a para llevar (take away) for our leftovers. Marlene teaches me Spanish words/phrases all the time which you find yourself using more and more frequently and recognising on menus, signs and all around. She is very knowledgeable.

After dropping them home, we got back, walked Bruno then had a lazy afternoon watching Christmas films. It was a very enjoyable day but I am getting a little lost; not having a routine of work or commitments is unnerving for me. I am going with the extended holiday idea in my head which enables me to cope with the current situation. We both have to find some form of work to cover our outgoings. It is so quiet here because of COVID, but then it is the same all over the world. Employment prospects are very slim and we have some time before we can depend on Pension payments coming in.

Monday 23rd November

On the agenda today after our usual morning routine is to open a bank account. I'm not too concerned about this as it should be a fairly easy procedure having acquired our NIE and Empadronamiento. So, we go off to our usual well-travelled place, Las Chafiras, as there are two banks side by side. Clive already has a Santander account in the UK so we assume it will be easier to go there. We were told it costs €40 a month because we are not yet residents so we decided to leave it a bit.

Clive rang the container company. Our items are due to be sent on 6/12/20. They should take about 10 days to arrive. He rang a guy about storage of our items and he is going to get back to us with a price.

Then, off to collect Clive's Citroen and pay the balance of the purchase price. Another simple procedure we thought. No. Clive's mobile banking wouldn't do international payments so he sent the €3,578.00 to my account. I then tried to pay that via my mobile banking app. No. I could only send up to €2,000 because it was a new payee. After the initial payment, you can then send up to €10,000 so, back tomorrow to pay the outstanding balance.

7.23 p.m. The payment still hasn't disappeared from my account. I went onto an online chat with Barclays. They said it could take up to 24 hours. I was advised that no charge would be taken for the transfer.

Clive called Santander and they talked him through the international payment process. You have to actually go online, not on your banking app.

Hopefully, we will get the hang of this as it is quite painful at the moment. I'm feeling a proper numpty.

Tuesday 24th November

As soon as I got up, I checked my banking app. The international payment had left my account. We went back to the car shop to pay the balance after Bruno had been for walkies and we all had breakfast. Then, off to sort out the car. Clive easily transferred the remainder of the balance. We now had to wait for it to be received then he could drive away in his "new work van" replacement 7-seater car if you get my meaning.

We went into Santander in Las Chafiras as we had to get a bank account to enable the residencia process. We waited over an hour in a long queue before entering the bank on our turn. When we got inside, we were handed a bank business card and told to message the contact on the card to make an appointment. They could not do it there and now; an appointment was required first to request a new bank account. We were handed a list of things required to open a bank account:—

- Rental contract / proof of residency
- Passport
- Proof of pension receipt
- NIE

The banks are obsessed with the fact you're getting a pension. Nothing seems to be straightforward in Tenerife.

Wednesday 25th November

We had a proper lazy day, not much to report other than the wonderful weather, sunny, blue skies, beautiful beach, clear water and still NO WORK. You would think most normal people would be grateful for the break but I do like a routine and one preferably that provides a positive effect on my bank balance, namely, work.

Thursday 26th November

Up and out to Clive's mum's. She checked over the form we had to complete for the Padrón tomorrow. She couldn't complete it online so we took it home to translate and complete.

We then went to Precios Al Alcance De Todo. Marlene recommended this shop for ink cartridges. We bought two for €27.80, one coloured and one black, which was a better deal than the last one we bought.

I drove Clive in our little hire car to collect his car. We then went and filled both the cars up with fuel which, by the way, is so much cheaper here than in the UK. On a Tuesday and Friday, it is on special. Diesel was 85 cents a litre and petrol 96 cents.

When we left the UK, diesel was £1.24 and petrol was £1.18. Huge difference. Yippee ki-yay……

We took the hire car back to the company. Clive picked me up and we went shopping. The usual outing to Mercadona.

Within 5 minutes of getting the Citroen, the reversing camera stopped working then Clive leant across on my armrest and snapped it clean off. It looks like a poor repair job had been carried out on the armrest. Oh well, now I'm in limp mode……

Luckily, the car comes with a year's warranty, and it turned out the camera was a simple loose cable. My armrest is still floating about in the back though. It doesn't fall under 'urgent repair' it turns out……

Friday 27th November

We got up about 6ish. It was still dark out when we walked Bruno. We were back by 7.45 a.m., then left to pick up Clive's mum and dad ready for our Padron meeting at 8.30. We got in there early. It was all Spanish, spoken rapidly so thank heavens for Marlene, yet again, coming to our rescue.

The forms required were:—contract for rental property, NIE, and passports. The lady took copies of our originals. The forms we had completed were not required. She filled forms in for us. We paid contactless €3 each and it was all done. It was a straightforward process if you can speak Spanish. We now have our Certificado de Empadronamiento.

The Great Brexit Exit

We left there and went for breakfast at about 9.10 a.m. Dropped Marlene and David back home then we decided to visit a dog-friendly beach at La Tejita for Bruno to have a paddle. It was lovely there and he met a lot of friendly dogs but just wasn't into the beach or water sadly. He is a proper spoilt pooch now……

This is where my daily scribblings become sporadic. I tend only to write down the things that I feel may be of interest. I really don't think that anybody wants to read about our extended holiday enjoyment when it's probably cold, wet, windy, maybe snowing back home and I'm harping on about the warmth of the sun, the beautiful scenery and clear stunning water, or the fact that since I've been here, my nails are longer and stronger than they have ever been. I feel so very lucky just getting here, to be honest, amongst the turmoil that is present the world over. Having been vitamin D deficient just before I left the UK and thus being on an intensive vitamin D supplement, I am getting everything I need from the sunshine here. I don't want to bang on about getting up every day to sunshine and blue skies but it is a way of life here. I would still have a job in the UK, as would Clive, but where we lived, the crime incidents were becoming increasingly commonplace and right on our doorstep. I feel safe here. You are able, not that we currently can because of COVID, to go out late at night and come home, slightly the worse for wear, merry shall we say, and feel safe. The police can utilise their force if need be and you don't get people abusing the police because they just wouldn't get away with it and I like it. In fact, I think everybody likes it. It's only the individuals requiring police intervention who would disagree. Obviously, COVID is to blame for unemployment rising, homelessness and deprivation leading to more crime, but at least the police force here are not reprimanded for doing their job. Human rights is not a reason to get away with being unlawful either verbally or physically.

On our day-to-day travels, we have met and continue to meet and chat to lots of people, some swallows (a phrase used to describe the pensioners who come here for the winter months) and ex-pats as well as Spanish people who speak English well. We glean as much information as we can from these people which has proved very helpful.

We found out about Autonomo for Clive which is self-employment and how to go about registering. Again, being self-employed here is nothing like in the UK. You have to contribute for three full years before you can sign off autónomo. You start paying €93 per month for the first 12 months; it then increases to €175 for 6 months then it increases again to €289 which is the most you have to pay. You pay tax every month regardless of whether or not you are earning. You must ensure you have the tax credit in your account or you will be fined and you will be eligible to pay the full tax amount for the entire year from there on in if you miss a payment. We were told everything we need to get our TIE cards. We had to make another appointment at the SAC office to obtain a Certificado de Convivencia (Coexistence Certificate) which proves we are living together/married. It is imperative to open a joint Spanish bank account. We have been trying with Santander but they won't allow you to make an appointment in the branch. We were given a business card and told to send a message explaining we needed an appointment to open an account. We messaged in English, no reply. Translated to Spanish, no reply. COVID restrictions have made some simple tasks infuriating, long-winded and laborious.

Sabadell next door was much easier to deal with since they have several English-speaking staff. The requirements regarding paperwork to open an account changed on each visit. It ranged from—proof of pension payments, NIE, passport, proof of address here and rental contract. On our next visit, we were asked for—passport, NI number, evidence of UK address, previous work contract. I had to ring Home Bargains and ask them to email my contract which they promptly did. Clive had to print his tax payments as he's always been self-employed.

Monday 7th December

We checked our post box and found our new Lobster SIM cards so returned home to ring Lobster and get our new numbers transferred to our mobiles which was a very simple procedure. We are now Spanish—well, our phones definitely are. Residency is still a work in progress.

Thursday 10th December

We arrived at the bank at 7.45 a.m., ready for opening at 8.15 a.m. You have to arrive early because of the queues. We were first in line. One person was waiting at Santander next door which was due to open at 8. He had a box to sit on. At 8.20, we went into Sabadell. The gentleman at the desk took and copied all our paperwork. He got us to fill in a form each. We were asked to return in the morning at 8.30 to open an account.

When we came out, Santander customers were still waiting outside. The branch should have opened before ours at 8 a.m. but they were still patiently waiting. Joke!

We have now got to wait for our health insurance confirmation and then we will be able to proceed online with our TIE.

Friday 11th December

We arrived at Sabadell for 8.20 a.m. They were just opening. A lady went in before us to see the gentleman dealing with new accounts so we had to wait. And wait we did; 45 minutes she was with our adviser. When she left, we got called in. All our paperwork was ready to sign. We had to pay €82 yearly to cover funeral expenses, etc. Because we are non-residents, we pay €40 per quarter for the banking service. When we have transferred the required €9,000 to be eligible for residency, we have to email to generate the

Certificado de Saldo (documents proving confirmation on the balance of our joint account). It takes 24 hours to generate the certificate then it can be emailed to us for our TIE application. The document is only valid for 48 hours so it will need to be forwarded straight on with our application.

After a quick lunch, we had our next appointment to obtain a Certificate to confirm we are living together. This is another requirement to get our TIEs. We arrived at 1.04 p.m., 4 minutes late at the SAC office because of heavy traffic in Las Chafiras. Luckily, the officials were both busy. We only waited about 2 minutes before we were called in. We handed the lady our translated request for the Certificado de Convivencia. She asked for our passports and a card payment of €3 then printed out our document proving we are living together. It took 5 minutes in total.

All we had to do now was transfer €9,000 to our Sabadell account and wait for the credit to be received. The transfer has been made; now we wait to see when it appears before requesting the Certificado.

We have to get the Health Insurance receipt, which is, I am told, in the pipeline, it is just very SLOW. Well, that isn't quite the full story. When it was time to pay for our health insurance, we were not in possession of our Spanish bank account and you can only pay with a Spanish bank account. Plus, it took about half a dozen phone calls before Clive actually got to speak to someone from the health insurance office. On the first few attempts, as soon as he spoke, the operative hung up on him. He really started to get cross about this and inventively translated 'No hablo español. Hay alguien que pueda hablar ingles por favor' so that he could play this in Spanish before they had a chance to hang up. Translated this means, 'I do not speak Spanish. Is there someone who can speak English, please?' Hey presto, it worked. He got put on hold and then an English-speaking person took over. It was all in vain anyway since we could not pay them. Clive spoke with the advisor who sold us the policy. He said if we transferred the money to him, he would pay the policy for us. I wasn't happy with this set-up but we had no choice. Clive transferred €1,610 for the full year's cover for both of us. The only trouble was, we found out after that we needed a receipt confirming we had paid. It had to have our names on, our NIE numbers and the bank account number it was paid from. Ah, we couldn't provide this as we hadn't paid from our account. I must admit, we did panic somewhat. After all the things we had obtained for our TIE application to progress, this may be the one thing preventing us from getting our Residency. Clive spoke to our rep again and he reassured him that a receipt would be forthcoming which would be acceptable for us to move forward. As is with most things here, a couple of days really means weeks or longer. The 'couple of days' for the receipt to arrive just kept getting longer, so, our poor rep did earn his wages on his sale to us because he was on speed dial on Clive's phone, and after another conversation, he managed to get the said receipt emailed so we could forward it on for our TIE. I think he must have been glad to see the back of us.

Wednesday 16th December

I found a plot of land for sale on one of the estate agent's sites that I check out regularly. The land was totally fenced off and footings had been laid with plumbing and electrics ready to go. The framework was on site with all the bathroom fittings and pipework. There were plans for the building to be erected—€50,000. We were both very interested and excited at the prospect of building our own place. There was still no work at the moment for us so it would have been the ideal time to take on a project like this. We had the finances to take this on and complete it, putting our own stamp on it.

I contacted the agent to make an appointment for viewing. It was at Las Galletas, at the edge of a plantation. Ideal, no neighbours, just banana plants. Lots of parking. I must admit, I was secretly dreaming of living there and had all the plans in my head of each room coming together.

The agent didn't get back to me straight away which isn't unusual. Two days later, I received an email notifying me that the plot had already been sold. Rowlocks!!!

Friday 18th December

I emailed our contact at Sabadell to order the Certificate confirming the balance of our account. It took 12 hours to issue so it should be with us on Monday 21st December. He confirmed he would email the Certificates on Monday.

Monday 21st December

I was still awaiting Sabadell's email but nothing so far. I am a very impatient person but I do not like pestering people so I did nothing about chasing it up then.

Tuesday 22nd December

I emailed Sabadell and was forwarded the Certificate immediately. I sent the paperwork on for our TIE which had to be in the system by 30/12/20.

Friday 25th December 2020

We had Christmas lunch at The Palms Restaurant. We all had a starter, roast dinner of our choice and dessert accompanied with wine. Festive crackers and Christmas cheer was present all around us with people smiling and laughing, exchanging pleasantries. It was a sunny, warm Christmas Day, so far away from our usual experience in England. We were all outside because of COVID restrictions but this was well received because of the weather. We were really spoilt. It was a glorious day with wonderful company.

8th January 2021

We decided it was time for me to get mobile ready for when Clive is working, then I'll be able to still get out and about, and hopefully find some kind of work myself. I saw a couple of cars I liked. I climbed in one and I didn't like the seat. Then I got in a Chevrolet Avero, took it for a test drive and bought it. It has to be serviced and get an ITV (MOT), so by the time they received my payment, it would be ready for me to collect. I couldn't believe I'd bought a car off the peg. It would usually take me ages and I'm normally very selective and fussy, insisting it needs to have low mileage and be immaculate, with one or two previous owners. That couldn't be any further from the case on this occasion. Not a clue how many previous owners it had and its mileage was fairly high; translating the kms, it had about 50,000 on the clock. It had several scratches and bruises. €5,000. Madness. No one looks after their cars here. They are all bruised and banged about. I don't think I'd like a brand-new car if I could afford it. On Clive's first trip to Mercadona in his Citroen, we came out with slightly more than we went in with. Someone rammed his car with a trolley. Unbelievable. He had several scars down the side from that unwanted collision. Then I drove straight into a column in the underground car park, adding to my collection of scars. 'Should have gone to SpecSavers' comes to mind, which I actually did, we both did in fact, just before leav-

ing the UK. I don't know what the hell happened there. All the columns are multicoloured with car paint from previous close encounters. It is something I am most careful with now, avoiding the bloody columns. Jeepers.

I think parking skills are not part of the driving test here…

Clive and I often look and laugh in amazement at cars that have been abandoned, not parked, literally left across two bays the wrong way or half on a zebra crossing; it's astonishing they have not received a ticket or been towed off.

5th January 2021

We saw a property advertised in Fasnia which looked quite interesting. It was a doer-upper but we thought we could take our time, design it, change it and extend it, so we requested a viewing. Neither of us had been to Fasnia before so we were looking forward to the experience. We were sent all the information via WhatsApp. It is the chosen message app used by virtually everybody here. That and Facebook. Rather than have Websites, a lot of companies advertise on Facebook. So, we set off after breakfast to Fasnia. It didn't take long before we were heading into the clouds. The altitude was something like 2,331m above sea level. I have become a proper pansy as I have matured. I didn't realise how frightened I would become driving up the steep roads, looking over the edge of the slim road at a vast plummeting abyss beside us and we weren't even at the height of our destination. I kept whining to Clive, begging him to slow down on the sharp bends as our ascent grew steeper and steeper. He found it amusing which angered me more and more as our climb became even more acute. When we got to within 2 minutes of the property, we had to park at the side of the road because the road which led into the property was at such an angle and steep descent, I was too scared to attempt the manoeuvre in the car. You couldn't see the road ahead of you because we were so steep, the car was angled at the sky. I was petrified so even before the viewing, I had decided, NOPE, this Fasnia was lunacy. There was no way I could make that drive let alone live there. Thank heavens I didn't take my car. It would have been a short trip because I would not have been able to get halfway there. Clive even agreed that the last leg of the journey had been horrible. We met with the estate agent, had a quick look around and told him thank you but no thank you. The altitude was just too much. The views were breathtaking because you were up in the gods. I know I was praying to get back down to the coast where I felt safe. If you lived here, you would have to step carefully; one wrong move and you'd be rolling downhill for miles to your death for sure. So, NOOOO to Fasnia. It was a no-brainer for sure.

11th February 2021

We saw an apartment advertised in Fraile. It was two bedrooms and looked really pleasant in the photographs online so we got an appointment once again. Fraile is near Las Galletas which is a place we visit often for brunch and a coffee. It is beautiful at Las Galletas. Fraile is a bit further inland and round the coast and has quite a few shops to browse around. We arrived at the property and had a bit of difficulty parking because it is quite a built-up area with blocks of flats. Not really our cup of tea but we continued with the tour since we had made an appointment. The estate agent took us into a tall block of flats, ground-floor property with a courtyard. It felt quite oppressive inside the building but we remained optimistic because the photographs of the apartment looked great. We entered and were deeply disappointed. The photographer should surely be in possession of a Pulitzer Prize for the pictures. They made the place look splendid when in fact it was a squat. We don't know how they did it but the rooms were small and the floors had been poorly repaired with pieces of tiles puzzled together. The pictures made the place look spacious, well maintained, sparkly and inviting which couldn't be any further from reality. This, like Fasnia, was a big No.

After this experience, we had no faith in the accompanying photographs provided by estate agents. It really put us off browsing through online agents. We just look when we are out and about, firstly, for the ideal location then a decent looking property, and also parking since we have two vehicles.

5th March 2021

I registered at the Hacienda tax office for a social security number for work. They are sending confirmation of that via email.

14th April 2021

Our appointment finally came through to attend at the Nacional de Policia in Santa Cruz at 10.00 a.m. to have our fingerprints taken for our TIE cards.

We got up early, walked Bruno and left home at 8.30 a.m. because we are both paranoid about being late. We deliberately work on being exceptionally early rather than 5 minutes late. We arrived in Santa Cruz well before our appointment time as parking is a big problem. We drove by the police station several times searching for a parking space. In the end, we agreed we would have to go further afield and walk back because we were getting closer and closer to our appointment time. As we were about to go onto the autopista, we saw an arrow for an underground parking lot. We managed to get a space fairly easily then made our way on foot to the police station. As it was, we had a little wait before being called in one at a time for the quick procedure of having our right-hand fingerprints taken. Once that was done, it was a waiting game. We had to keep checking online to see when our lot numbers for our cards would be ready for collection.

26ᵗʰ April

We made an appointment to attend Centro de Reconocimiento de Conductores at Las Chafiras for our health certificates which are a requirement for changing our English driving licences to Spanish. We were told beforehand by some friends that it was nothing to worry about. It was quite a simple procedure; a quick eye test then we had to sit at a computer screen and use two joy sticks, one in each hand, directing two circles along two separate winding roads. The roads went in two different directions and each time you touched the edge of the road or went outside of the lines, the machine bleeped. It wasn't the only thing that bleeped. So, you had one eye in York, one eye in Cork, trying to drive down two separate roads winding in different directions. Very strange on the grey matter. Hand/eye coordination testing at its best/worst. Luckily, we both passed. Oh, we were also asked if we were mental, to which I lied and said NO, and also if we abused alcohol or drugs. Quite strange—Cost of test—€35 each.

So, we were now in receipt of confirmation of our TIE having attended for fingerprints. This confirmation took the form of a stamped letter which was required to proceed with the transfer of the driving licences. This was being dealt with for us at a cost of €50 each. The transfer of the licences cost €30 each. We had to hand in our plastic driving licences and a copy of our passport. Another item ticked off our 'To-Do List'. It was a six to eight-week wait until we received our new Spanish driving licences.

30th April—1st May

We were off on holiday whilst on holiday. (It still felt like a holiday to be honest, not like we lived there yet. It was surreal).

Clive's parents asked us if we wanted to go to Puerto de la Cruz for a long weekend. Why, of course, was the tandem reply.

The north of the island is so lush and green. They get much more rain than the south. It is glorious there but then the whole island is. So, we were booked into the Monopol, all three of us, Clive, myself and Bruno in one room. Yep, Bruno had a holiday on holiday too. Clive's mum and dad and a couple of their friends were also going. The hotel was lovely and really reasonable. The weekend flew by and we all had a fantastic time, relaxing, eating and drinking far too much, us three anyway.

While we were there, we all visited The Botanical Gardens. I overloaded my iPhone with a few hundred pictures. Far too many to load onto here, but the plants, flowers and trees—everything was phenomenal.

We did so much walking and took in so many floral breathtaking sites.

20th May 2021

There had been several reports on the radio about COVID vaccinations locally so, after speaking with Marlene (not only Clive's mother but a very competent translator which is imperative to advancing with anything on this island), she thought it would be best to actually go to the medical centre rather than ring as they had been inundated with people trying to book in. We picked them up and drove to Las Chafiras medical centre.

We arrived about 10.30 a.m. We waited a short while and were told, via Marlene translating, to go onto San Isidro hospital as they had been overwhelmed.

We travelled onto San Isidro. We were directed to various doors and the third door was the winner. We had our temperatures checked, were directed to the hand sanitiser and given different face masks as ours were not up to standard. Marlene did all the communicating again. Our paperwork was taken and appointments were made. June 1st Los Cristianos, Clive 3.12 p.m., me 3.24 p.m.

Marlene also informed us we had to renew our Certificado de Empadronamiento. It only lasts 6 months. This registers you at your local town hall. If you move, you have to update this information.

When we got back home, I went online and got us an appointment at the SAC office for 27th May at 8 a.m., so we could renew the form.

27th May

We attended the SAC office and renewed the appropriate form for us both. €3 each. It didn't take long. We had a quick Spanish brush up on our iPhones before going in so that we didn't look like total muppets. The lady spoke a little English, so, between our handful of words and hers, it wasn't too painful.

Could this be our forever home? Please………

Clive and I fell in love with this property when we first saw it. Apparently, it has been empty for years. We had looked at various properties since we arrived. As yet, we hadn't had the feeling we experienced when we saw this place so we thought we would try and find out who owned it, if they wanted to sell it, and, most importantly, if it was in our budget. I wrote to our local Town Hall, in Spanish, with the address and this picture, to find out who owned it. A few weeks later, there was an official

Correos notice in our post box. We had to go to the main post office with the note within 7 days of receipt. Today (the day I collected it from our post box), was day 7 so we had to drive straight there. I had to produce my Passport, NIE, sign two official documents, one of them digital, then finally, I was handed a letter. It was from the Town Hall. I translated it. It advised us to go to the Town Hall in Arona so we drove there. We were met by an official who, obviously, spoke thick Spanish. We gathered (by which, I mean, stupidly assumed), the office was shut and we would have to go back Monday morning (this being late Friday).

We returned on Monday morning. Third in line to go in. The people in front all spoke Spanish and were dealt with promptly. We faced the official who asked us something, doh…, the guy who had been in front of us and was waiting for something on the sidelines kindly translated as he spoke very good English…, 'you need an appointment'. We thanked him and promptly left, tail between our legs!

Why didn't we realise that everything required an online appointment request? Back to the trusted iPhone and we had an appointment for that Thursday.

Thursday arrived—Clive explained, with the help of his iPhone, what we wanted. The lady explained we would need to go online to the Land Registry and request the information. So, we returned home, went on the iPad and did exactly as we were told; completed the form, paid the €60 administration fee and waited. Clive then received an email saying that our application had been rejected due to the lack of information provided. As yet, we are still none the wiser. We need to find someone in the know.

You don't realise just how debilitating it is not having any communication skills. Holidaying here is fine. You can get away with not being able to speak Spanish. The staff in most of the holiday resorts have a reasonable grasp of most languages. The waiters/waitresses speak several languages most of the time. It is when it comes to living here and going to hospital, doctors, council, police that you need to know the basics in Spanish.

Clive and I embarked on Spanish lessons. We managed to squeeze 4 lessons in before work took off. I say 'took off' loosely as, unfortunately, it quickly plummeted. That enabled us to say our names, address, date of birth and phone numbers in Spanish. We can order drinks and some food but anything official and we fall short of being able to communicate successfully. Most people take an interpreter to appointments or pay for professional help when it comes to securing residency. It really can leave you feeling despondent, stupid, 'weighed, measured and found wanting', to coin a phrase I find very satisfying. I sit and ponder what on earth must have been bouncing around in my somewhat empty brain. Why didn't we prepare ourselves properly? We really should have started learning Spanish in England.

Tuesday 1ˢᵗ June 2021

Marlene arranged to go with us for our COVID jabs in case we needed her translating skills. David had a 2.30 p.m. appointment at his doctor's so, the plan was to pick them up, go for lunch, take David to his 2.30 appointment then go onto Mahon Hospital for our jabs. We picked them up at noon, drove to Servelyns at Parque la Reina, ordered our tapas and waited. Unfortunately, they were quite busy and the wait was lengthy so by the time our food arrived, it was almost 2 p.m. We ended up being a little late for David's appointment. He was kept waiting so by the time we got to Mahon Hospital, our appointment times of 3.12 and 3.24 had already expired. It was gone 3.30 p.m. None of us like being late but it was out of our hands and, luckily for us, there was a small queue of people waiting for their jab. No mention was made of our lateness. We were sent to another queue and then received our vaccine. We had the one-off Janssen, the Johnson & Johnson brand. It was all very civilised and didn't take long at all. We had to wait for 15 minutes afterwards to ensure there were no ill effects. Whilst sitting, we were called by name and handed our stamped Certificate to prove we had the vaccine. I think we gave up after 10 minutes then walked round to where Marlene and David were quenching their thirst with a coffee. We sat and joined them for a coffee then headed back to drop them home before returning to our apartment to take Bruno out.

Wednesday and Thursday turned out to be not too pleasant for us. We both had headaches, waves of nausea, aching muscles, upset stomachs and generally felt washed out. We started to feel better by Friday but took things easy.

Several people had told us that having side effects was a good thing as it meant your body was producing antigens. We reasoned we would be fine because I think we ticked the box of every side effect listed on the Janssen site.

4th June 2021

We bit the bullet and made arrangements to view a three-bedroom apartment in Los Abrigos. It is a beautiful area right on the coast which is what we like, not up in the gods. The apartment was a little smaller than we would have liked but pleasant enough. It was the parking once again that put us off. We drove around for 10 minutes trying to find a space. Luckily, on our second circuit of the area, we happened across someone just leaving a space so we moved in quickly. Once again, we decided that was too big a downfall. Where we are, we have ample parking for both vehicles and even though we are renting, we are happy to continue until we find something which is more suitable.

13th June 2021

Clive and I took the water bottles to the machine on-site to refill. The machine filters out all the bad elements making the tap water drinkable. It costs 10 cents a litre which is cheaper than buying bottled. Whilst we were there, we went to our post box which is in a large bank of post boxes for the whole complex. We only remember to check our postbox when we refill our water bottles because they are in the same location. Sometimes we bring the wrong keys and can't be bothered to walk back to the apartment so, all in all, we don't visit it as often as we should but then we don't receive the volume of post we did in the UK so it isn't on our list of priorities. To our surprise, there were two envelopes, one for Clive, the other for me. They were our new Spanish driving licences. So, we are good for 9 years now until the next renewal.

Marlene sent me a link about TIE cards which showed that our numbers were ready for collection. We planned to drive to Santa Cruz the following week to collect them. That was the last piece of the puzzle needed for residency.

Wednesday 23rd June

I double-checked on the website about our TIE cards and we had to collect them before 1st July since after that date, you were required to make an appointment. We decided today was the day for our long-awaited trip. We walked Bruno early so we could be on our way. We arrived just after 10 a.m. and were unable to get near the underground car park. The traffic was backed up waiting to get in. We drove around for a while and decided to return to the underground parking area as everywhere else was jammed solid. When we got there, we drove down the ramp which was now empty, collected our ticket from the machine and spent 10 minutes finding a space. At least we managed to find one and since we could arrive at any time, there was no panic this time round. We walked to the police station, waited just a few minutes before our paperwork was taken and I was led in first. My card was brought to me, my prints were taken again and I was dismissed with my new TIE card in hand. Clive was next. He was met by a different officer who asked him for his green card, which we did not have, then his passport.

Strange; I was not asked for either. Crime Watch sprung to mind fleetingly. My next thought was could I find my way home alone? Tehehehe!

Finally, he emerged after what seemed like a long time. He jokingly said, "They won't let me in; I've been refused." He's a little s… Wind-up. He did get his card.

So, we were now officially RESIDENTS! Currently unemployed. Well, I was unemployed. Clive was awaiting work. As I have said, he cannot sign off until he has paid into the system for 3 years so we were hoping the situation would improve and we would both get something since we have no income at present.

It is worth noting that in Spain, if you see anybody wandering around with a file, they are either going to the police, hospital, bank or the Council Offices, as these require ALL your paperwork. Also, for your Spanish Bank, you need a Spanish mobile number as I have already said but you need it for other entities too. Everyone has a mobile, not everyone has a landline. Your SIM card is registered through the police, as is your car. You always need to produce your NIE number for any official procedure and for buying some goods.

You do not require a landline to receive Wi-Fi. This is a big con in the UK, allowing phone companies to charge for landlines when they are no longer needed by most households. I find it ludicrous.

If you want to stay here, you need a permanent address to register with the Padron (Council Offices) in order to qualify for residency, and with the police for NIE, TIE, anything official really. The forms can be downloaded online, completed and printed, then tax paid at the bank before registering them at the appropriate office.

It is imperative that you have a translation app if you do not speak Spanish. This has saved our lives on many occasions as, if you don't help yourself, most Spanish officials will not willingly offer to speak English or whatever language you speak, yet, if you make the effort to speak even a handful of words, they are more likely to be helpful.

We have met so many friendly, helpful people since we arrived who have provided us with information. Some has been invaluable, some just noteworthy, some you have to file in your brain under "To Avoid Unwanted Police Attention and possibly a fine", i.e., your dog must not be off the lead and running around near public roads—this carries a fine; you are not allowed to wash your car on the road—this carries a fine. You can, however, wash it on your own private property if you have a garden or drive. Not wearing a face mask carries a €200 on the spot fine.

Although, thankfully, as of the 26th of June this year, face masks do not have to be worn outside. If you go into a shop or an enclosed area, then they have to be worn. Who knows when this will change? We were on Stage 2 not so long ago, but now, as numbers of infected rise in Santa Cruz, Stage 3 has come into effect once again restricting numbers at restaurant tables to 4. This will continue to be a fluid situation, one we will all have to continue to change with.

20th July 2021

Face masks must now be worn outside when it is impossible to be a safe distance from other people. You must always carry a face mask; you will be fined €500 if you are without one.

16th/17th/18th August

This has been our first experience of extremely high temperatures. A Calima and Sirocco combined cause extreme heat, high winds and a feeling like no other. Since Monday 16th August, the thermometer has been up to 47 degrees. We were prewarned that it would feel like you were in an oven or someone had turned a hairdryer on full blast.

Hmmmmm. I think we clocked up three showers, three trips to the swimming pool and more changes of clothes than I can remember. The only other time comparable to this was when we holidayed in Portugal. We were out driving in our hire car, aircon on full blast. Clive suggested turning it off and opening our windows for some fresh air. That lasted about 10 seconds as we found it hard to breathe, it was so damned hot. This weather front made a simple task like walking a sweaty, drippy hell. My face was damp and droplets of sweat trickled down my back into my underwear. Far from pleasant. Talk about limp lettuces. It drained the energy as well as the fluid from your body. I don't know about Clive but I felt like a shrivelled prune. Bruno also had to have several showers to cool off. I bought orange and lemon ice lollies to quench our thirst. Bruno sat staring whilst we consumed these frozen treats so I tried him with a small piece. To my amazement, he lapped it up. In fact, he ended up eating a whole one chopped into small pieces and, thus far, has consumed more than us. It certainly aided in cooling him down for quite some time. After this heat, we concluded that our own place will have air conditioning in the main living area and bedroom. The Spanish were still working in long trousers and t-shirts. Unbelievable. I know we still need time to acclimatise, but long trousers? I'll never be in those even when I've been here 5 years. That's just wrong.

This is not the end; far from it. Our journey continues, as will my notes, and maybe an update on adventures if a dream of mine is realised and the amazing happens—self-publish first, then actually sell this, my work.

Until the next time,

    Lisa, Clive and Bruno 🐾 🐾

As promised, our total expenditure for our travel over is as follows:—

Tolls—€146.10   Diesel—€246.98

Totalling—€393.08 (through France only)

I feel a need to mention specific people who have come into my life and impacted me. They do not realise their worth for me. Each and every one has enabled me to move on with my journey and new life. I thank you……

Marlene, David, Diane, Will, Nita, Tracey, Aaron, Tash, the Lamms and everyone who befriended me at HB. I miss you and hope you make the trip over soon.

To my new acquaintances who encouraged me, Dawn and Lorna.

And to my son, Shaun; your advice and technology head have been invaluable.

www.ingramcontent.com/pod-product-compliance
Lightning Source LLC
Chambersburg PA
CBHW070915080526
44589CB00013B/1306